The Couples' Guide to Money

The Couples' Guide to Money

Linda Gough

ALLEN&UNWIN

First published in 2004

83 Alexander Street,
Crows Nest NSW 2065 Australia
Phone: (61 2) 8425 0100
Fax: (61 2) 9906 2218
E-mail: info@allenandunwin.com
Web: www.allenandunwin.com

National Library of Australia
Cataloguing-in-Publication entry:

Gough, Linda.
The couples' guide to money: how to make the most of your financial power as a couple.

Includes index.
ISBN 1 86508 949 4
1. Finance, Personal. 2. Married people—Finance, Personal.
3. Unmarried couples—Finance, Personal. I. Title.

332.0240655

Set in 11/13 pt Garth Graphic by Midland Typesetters, Maryborough, Vic.

10 9 8 7 6 5 4 3 2 1

Contents

Acknowledgments x
Foreword John Eales xi

1 **The power of two 1**
Double the strength 2
When love is new 2
Quarrels about money 3
The bottom line 5

2 **Goals to get started 6**
What is your financial personality profile? 7
What is your combined financial profile? 8
Your values—what is really important to you? 13
Your dreams 13
Your attitudes 14
Your goals 15
Achieving your aims 15
How many goals at one time? 18

3 **Get help to build wealth 20**
Finding the right adviser 21
How to interview an adviser 23
What's it going to cost? 24
What do you take with you? 24
How much risk is tolerable? 26
Be demanding 26
Keep an eye on your plan 27
When to change advisers 27

4 **Taking control of debt 32**
Debt can ruin your health 33
Are we really in serious debt? 34

How couples get into debt 35
Sexually transmitted debt 35
Impulse buying 38
Credit cards 40
Store cards 41
Mobile phones 42
Living beyond your means 42
Interest rate hikes 44
Addiction problems 44
A partner's debts 45
Christmas—keep it jolly 46
Bankruptcy dilemma 48

5 The blueprint for budgeting 49
When it's time for a budget 50
Where does our money go? 50
Spend one income, save the other 51
How to draw up a budget 52
How to save an extra $300 a month 54
Ultimate budgeting tips 56
Mobile phone checklist 58
The cost of credit 60
Your children's education 62

6 Be winners on one wage 65
Practise living on one income 66
Paying the mortgage 68
How to ask your partner for money 70
Honey, can we afford the kids? 70
Your child care options 72
Income protection insurance 76

7 Dealing with baggage 77
Who pays for what? 78
Pre-existing assets 79
Pre-nuptial agreements 79
Separate versus joint accounts 81
Whose house to live in 83
Children come first 83

Maintenance matters 84
Demands for more 86
The costs keep coming 87

8 Get rich with bricks 89
Can you afford it? 90
Your home loan choices 91
Get help to get the right loan 94
Pay off your mortgage faster 95
Your dream home 97
Research, research, research 98
Before you buy 99
Before the auction 99
At the auction 100
Make an offer 100
Legal affairs 101
What if your partner already has a mortgage? 102
Tenants in common/joint tenants 102
Investment property 102
Off the plan 104
Deposit bonds 104
Renting versus buying 105
Buying versus renovating 107
Listed property trusts 109

9 How to make loads from a little 113
What are our choices for investing? 114
Managed funds 117
Ethical funds 119
Emerging markets 120
Master trusts 120
Wrap accounts 121
Ten tips for smart investing 122

10 All about shares 130
How much do we need? 131
Can we buy and sell shares in joint names? 131
Should we buy shares in the name of
the lower earner? 131

Can we take out a joint loan to buy shares? 132
How do we select which shares to buy? 132
When do we buy and sell shares? 133
What are discount brokers? 134
What is a buy-back offer and when should you accept it? 135
Some super share tips 136
What is margin lending? 140
Who should consider a margin loan? 140
What is a margin call? 140

11 Get the max from tax 142
Six ways to trim your tax 143
Seek help 149
Use an accountant 150
Lodging your return 151
Salary sacrificing for same-sex couples 151
End-of-year tax schemes 152
Family tax benefits 153
Baby bonus 154
The claim game 154
Capital gains tax 156
Family trusts 157

12 Take the super highway 159
What's so great about super? 160
How much super do we need? 161
A tale of two incomes 162
Your super choices 163
Seven super strategies 167

13 Take cover 177
Put family first 177
Safeguard your income 179
Don't neglect your health 181
Ease the trauma 183
Contents count 184
The little extras 185

14 Where there's a will . . . 188
Who should make a will? 189
How to make a will 189
What happens if you die without a will? 190
How to choose an executor 190
The cost of a will 191
What revokes a will? 193
The tax benefits of trusts 193
Who can contest a will? 194
Where to keep your will 194
De facto and same-sex couples 194
The law prevails 195
The final word 195

15 When love goes wrong 197
Heal your heart 198
Seek advice 198
Honesty is the best policy 199
Put finances first 201
Change your priorities 201
Divorce alternatives 202
If you go to court 203
Property settlements 203
The cost of going to court 205
Timing the settlement 206
Settle out of court 206
The de facto factor 207
Calculating child support 210
Be savvy about super 210
Legal aid 211
Family trusts 212
Personal gifts 212
Same-sex couples 212

Conclusion 214

Appendix 1: Personal Money Plan 216

Index 219

Acknowledgments

I was fortunate to have a number of people helping me on this, my first book. Thanks to Rob Coombe for having the faith in me to write it and supporting me the whole way through. I could not have written the book without my researcher, editor and motivator, Jane-Anne Lee, who is an accomplished journalist and writer in her own right. To my loving husband for his confidence and pride in me and to my young son, Wil, who stood at the bottom of the stairs on the days I worked at home and waved goodbye to me through his tears: thankyou. Thanks also to my Mum, who proudly tells everyone she has an author in the family!

A special thankyou to all the experts who gave up their valuable time to talk to me and to the staff at BT Financial Group who provided essential feedback. To the *Sun-Herald* for its continued support of me and my column and to my publishers, Allen & Unwin, for their enthusiasm and commitment to the project.

But most of all I want to thank my Dad for instilling in me his amazing values and the importance of having life goals. He is an absolute inspiration to me and gave me the confidence to never give up on my dreams.

Foreword

Lara and I have only been married now for four years but in that time we have encountered any number of financial decisions, each of which has required us to work together as a team.

Fundamental decisions, like the sale of one house and the purchase of another, the organising of wills, the purchase of various insurances and household budgeting can create complex and emotional issues that require a lot of considered and technical discussion. That being the case, they are often decisions that couples are not always suitably informed to make on their own.

Two things have helped us enormously over that period of time. One of those has been the help of experts and the other is the fact that we have worked together as a team.

Effective teams share a vision of the journey and destination that they wish to embark on together. They set goals that clearly stipulate the roles and responsibilities each member of the team has in order for the team to arrive at its destination. They communicate effectively and with empathy for each of the members of the team. They remain composed no matter how daunting the circumstances might seem. And very importantly, they respect the various strengths and weaknesses of all the individuals in the team because at the end of the day it is the people within the team that make up the team itself.

Significantly, life in a team is very different and a whole lot better than life on your own—that is, I should add, if you are in a good team. People put an enormous amount of work into their sporting teams, or their business teams, but often neglect the most important team that they are involved in—the one with their life partner.

Financial decisions can be a lot more complex as part of a team than they may be for an individual. Equally, though, the achievements of the team can be so much more rewarding than the achievements of an individual. Linda Gough's book, *The Couples' Guide to Money,* recognises all these facts about teams and guides you through the process in a very easily digestible way.

This book doesn't try to preach to you about what you should be doing (everybody hates that); instead, it actually goes about giving you practical examples of how you *can* do it. The author guides you throughout the book with suggestions of how you can work as a team in the decision-making process.

It is a book about practicalities that everyone encounters in life and can be read in its entirety or used as a reference point for future financial decisions.

No matter what your financial competence may be, by the time you have finished reading this book, you will have gained something from within its pages. It may be just a confirmation that you are on track, or a reminder that there is work to be done; for a few it may save your finances as well as your relationship.

Sit back and enjoy the book, but most importantly learn the lessons, because to be forewarned is to be forearmed and if you plan now you won't have to pay later.

John Eales
Sydney, 2004

1

The power of two

Myth: Love conquers all.
Fact: You wish—money matters are the main source of arguments in relationships.

Remember those first heady months of your relationship when money was the furthest thing from your mind? You both thought that it would all sort itself out. Anyway, who needs money when you are in love?

If only things would stay like that forever. As we all know, relationships mature and inevitable life decisions begin to surface whether we like it or not, especially when children enter the equation. Decisions such as: Do we need to buy a property instead of renting? Should we start an investment portfolio? And do we need one bank account or two, or even three—mine, yours and ours?

The aim of this book is to guide you through the challenges of life as a couple—and by couple I mean married, de facto or same-sex. I am also aiming to help you gain security together, emotionally and financially, so that you can enjoy life to the full. There are chapters on goals, budgeting, financial planning, dealing with emotional baggage, getting out of debt, buying property and much more.

There is even a chapter to help you with financial issues in the event of splitting up.

Money alone doesn't bring you happiness, but it sure helps. Money can give you the freedom to make more choices in life so you can plan that overseas holiday together rather than dream about it, buy a home instead of renting and take control of your financial future. In other words, it can help give you your desired 'lifestyle'—the buzzword for young couples, as social researcher Hugh Mackay told me:

> What young couples are trying to do these days is create for themselves a way of life that actually reflects their values. They look at older people, especially their own parents, and they say, well their lives didn't actually reflect their values, they didn't spend enough time with each other, they didn't have enough downtime, they didn't make enough changes, they got into a rut, they worked too hard, they drank too much, they bought too much stuff. They are thinking about meaning and purpose in their lives in non-material ways as well as material. I think 'lifestyle' is a good term because it conveys the idea that they are still heavily into material possessions, but they think that there is more to life.

DOUBLE THE STRENGTH

You don't have to be a rocket scientist to appreciate that the earning power of two is twice as strong as the earning power of one. Couples who decide to get serious about their future together will no longer have to pay separate rent, fork out for two food bills, have two household insurance policies and so on.

While many of the cost savings of being in a partnership are obvious, others are not so apparent. For example, by combining investments and using the power of two salaries, a team of two can borrow more easily for a much larger home and have far greater flexibility to pay it off faster.

But the most rewarding outcome of investing as a couple is that when two people work together to accomplish a goal, they can usually achieve it twice as fast. This can only make the journey to financial security more enjoyable.

WHEN LOVE IS NEW

In the beginning, couples share all sorts of secrets with each other. Yet, while you may talk intimately with your partner about many things, you can often be worried or embarrassed about discussing money matters.

This may be fine in the early stages of your relationship—the fact that your loved one is a big spender or is mad about betting at the races might initially be considered only slightly annoying or even cute. However, if certain habits which are merely irritating at the start of a relationship are left to fester, they will undoubtedly become big issues as the partnership matures.

According to the counselling group Relationships Australia, the main causes of strain and tension in a relationship are money, work and children—in that order.

QUARRELS ABOUT MONEY

Couples argue about all sorts of issues relating to money. They may be living beyond their means; they may not be saving enough; they may have made poor investments or they may simply be pathetic money managers. There can be other problems too.

One partner may earn more than the other, creating feelings of guilt and resentment. But, as Melbourne psychologist Meredith Fuller said in our interview:

> There are many ways of adding currency in your relationship. For example, the one who earns less money may do more of the bill paying and organise the social calendar.
>
> Dollar superiority is a risky position in these economic times because things can change dramatically. One partner can get retrenched or fall ill so it's always dangerous to assume that the one who has the higher earning capacity will always call the tune.
>
> In terms of the relationship, you both need to get clear from the outset what the value of your contribution is and not just look at it in dollar terms. You should also determine how you will make key decisions and have a rule that you will discuss big purchases together beforehand.

One partner may be a spender, the other a saver. Fuller says people generally tend to manage their money according to the way their parents did—either by copying them or by doing the complete opposite:

> If he comes from a family of savers and she comes from a family of splurgers, they both need to sit down and work out how to create a new set of family rules. Neither is right nor wrong; they are just different. Each may believe that the other is demonstrating a lack of consideration and lack of love, but it isn't about this at all.
>
> One of you is absolutely convinced that the spender can't truly love them because they are blowing all their money and the other one thinks the saver can't truly love them because they are so mean and withholding. If you reach that stalemate, it may be time to visit a couples' counsellor.

You may be in a relationship where you are always paying the bills or bailing out your other half—but have you teamed up with a partner or a pet? Life is about give and take, and you want to avoid static patterns such as this where you will end up resenting one another.

If your partner has financial ties to a past relationship, this can also be a source of resentment, frustration, jealousy and guilt which will need to be addressed. This is discussed further in Chapter 7.

You may be living together but spending as though you were both single. It is possible that you have a commitment problem you are reluctant to confront. However, if you want to take advantage of the real power of two, you need to work out what you both want from life, where you are prepared to compromise—and where you aren't.

Couples with a similar vision for the future tend to avoid money arguments, but the reality is that many couples have slightly different views on what money means and what their intentions are. You need to find a win–win solution *together*.

To have a successful financial future as a couple, it is also essential to learn how to balance living an enjoyable life with some form of saving and still splurge now and then.

THE BOTTOM LINE

If you have bought this book to get rich quick, you will be disappointed. If you have bought it to help you get rich together, then you are on the right track. Creating sustainable wealth as a couple is about:

- working together as a team and discussing your values—it is difficult to set goals unless you discuss what your values are;
- setting goals—be realistic and celebrate your achievements;
- creating a plan and writing it down—developing a plan without writing it down is a recipe for failure;
- saving and investing often—investing in the sharemarket does not require a large amount of money. The most important aspect is to save and invest on a regular basis in amounts you can comfortably afford;
- starting today—don't use the excuse that you can't afford to start because you have too many debts. The sooner you start, the sooner you will reach your goals—even if it means that the first year of your plan is spent paying off your debts.

The message is that any couple can be financially secure and successful. The key is to work together to achieve your goals, communicate often with each other on how comfortable you are with your plans, check your progress regularly and above all enjoy life and your successes along the way.

Treat money matters as you would any other issues in your relationship—with care, love and attention. Couples' counsellors even suggest that you should run your relationship like a small business, constantly monitoring its performance.

Some of the concepts in this book may seem a little confronting. Please don't be put off. Couples who take the time to talk about life's most important issues will know where they stand with one another, and there will rarely be nasty surprises. Remember, what is important to you may not be important to your partner. The key is to find common ground and to learn to compromise for the health of the relationship.

2

Goals to get started

Myth: You don't need to set financial goals. Just save as much as you can.

Fact: Goals give you direction and help make your dreams a reality.

Your personality shapes so much of your life. It helps to determine the type of car you drive, the clothes you wear, the partner you choose, the arguments you have, the house you buy, the renovations you carry out and the investments you make.

Personality is the driving force. You control it, but sometimes it can take a back seat or develop a life of its own, especially if you are in a relationship with a different personality type. Of course, you shouldn't despair if you and your partner do happen to be at opposing ends of the personality spectrum. One often helps to balance out the other. For example, instead of buying that totally impractical convertible car at the same time as planning a first child, a steadier personality will steer a partner towards car yards selling four-door sedans or station wagons. On the flip side, a holiday kayaking down a raging river can turn any conservative personality into lots of fun!

When it comes to money, our financial personalities may be different again. However, it doesn't matter what type of financial personality you are—you and your partner will probably have different attitudes about money. Your partner may be a control freak who needs to take charge of your finances. Or a high roller who enjoys taking risks but has no interest in the finer details of investing or even considering how much is at stake. Or your partner may prefer a slow, steady road when you want to take the freeway!

Consider the following questions. How are you at saving money as a couple? Who sets the savings agenda? Do you argue over credit card statements or splurges on those little luxuries in life? Is one partner a big spender who never looks at price tags while the other keeps track of every cent?

Be aware that the most common financial personality combination with couples is a hoarder and a spender. If not dealt with properly and maturely, this issue can easily turn into the one you argue about the most. Remember, money is the single biggest point of contention for couples.

Knowing your financial personality type and what makes you and your partner tick will help in making the right financial moves and setting the sort of goals that will work for both of you. Along the way, your relationship will be the big winner as you learn how a small change in your behaviour—or even an awareness of *why* you are the way you are—can help to establish and achieve your combined goals.

WHAT IS YOUR FINANCIAL PERSONALITY PROFILE?

Take the first step to financial success by having a bit of fun with the following matching game. First, try deciding what financial personality profile you *best* fit. Then match yours with that of your partner and see what challenges and opportunities you can create together as a couple.

Are you a thrillseeker?

You enjoy taking risks—from acting on a share tip from your best friend's neighbour to investing in your brother-in-law's Internet company. You may have a short attention span and tend to be enthusiastic about life and all it has to offer. You have limited patience and aren't too fussed about detail—all you want is the bottom line. You also want to become rich as fast as you can. When it comes to spending, it's all about easy come, easy go. If you see something you like, you must have it, regardless of the price tag.

Are you savvy?

You have always been switched on about money matters and have probably had a share portfolio or investment property since you were aged in your twenties. You are a goal-setter from way back. You like your money to be working for you so you always keep an eye on returns. You often do your own research but are more than happy to seek out good advice in order to get you where you want to be. When you do take a risk, you do it with confidence.

Are you steady?

When it comes to detail, you can't get enough. You almost bury yourself in it. Before making a decision, you do plenty of research, weighing up all the pros and cons. You like to feel comfortable about your finances so you can sleep at night. You prefer the known to the unknown. You are a 'blue-chip' kind of person, preferring consistent returns with an established track record, and you manage your credit cards brilliantly.

Are you timid?

When it comes to investing, you believe you can't go past owning your own home. You find it difficult to cope with risk. You like to put your money in the bank and leave it there. You don't particularly like shares because you feel they can be too volatile and you don't want to entertain the possibility of losing your hard-earned money. You also like predictability, so guaranteed returns have the most appeal.

WHAT IS YOUR COMBINED FINANCIAL PROFILE?

Once you and your partner have determined your respective financial profiles, combine the two to see what's in store for the both of you.

Thrillseeker + savvy

Pitfalls

Thrillseeker has the potential to frustrate savvy by taking one too many risks. Equally, savvy will try to rein in thrillseeker's enthusiasm by demanding to see the facts and figures behind that latest scheme to make millions. Be prepared for stormy arguments!

Positives

Both of you are keen to make money and prepared for some element of risk. Savvy should be able to temper thrillseeker's extravagance with some commonsense logic and hard-nosed facts. Thrillseeker can possibly persuade savvy to loosen the purse strings and make quicker decisions about that investment.

Thrillseeker + steady

Pitfalls

This is a potential battleground. Steady will find it difficult to convince thrillseeker to read the five newspaper articles warning against their latest scheme. Thrillseeker will have a million reasons why you both should go ahead, while steady refuses to budge.

Positives

Over time, and with perseverance and some heated debate, steady may be able to sway thrillseeker to take a middle road instead of the high ground. Thrillseeker can help steady mellow a little and agree to some level of calculated risk in their portfolio.

Thrillseeker + timid

Pitfalls

A challenging combination! Let's get one thing clear neither of you will be able to have what you really want. Compromise is necessary to achieve harmony. The danger is that timid will be unable to hose down thrillseeker's enthusiasm and thrillseeker will take charge and just do it.

Positives

Effective communication, and lots of it, will be the key along with a good financial planner who understands your diverse risk profiles. Thrillseeker will be forced to compromise while timid must accept that a little risk is a good thing.

Thrillseeker + thrillseeker

Pitfalls

This can be a potentially dangerous combination! No one will curb your unbridled enthusiasm. You will be so excited about the next big opportunity that goal-setting and planning will go out the window. Separate agendas may be recklessly pursued.

Positives

It's never a dull moment in a relationship where life is full of money-making possibilities. It's all about going for growth regardless of risk. Money will be made and lost and made and lost again. Whenever you are down, you will always believe that you can bounce back.

Savvy + savvy

Pitfalls

There aren't too many pitfalls here. But you may share different, but strong, unwavering opinions on how to achieve success. Be prepared to concede that you may both be right when it comes to setting your investment strategy. The odd compromise may be required.

Positives

You pay off credit cards in full each month. You are keen to make money through goal-setting and smart financial planning. Decisions about your finances will be backed up with sound investment strategies.

Savvy + steady

Pitfalls

Savvy may be tempted by steady's desire for detail and consequently miss out on opportunities that require snappy decisions. Conversely, savvy may become frustrated by steady's cautious nature and want to take bigger risks.

Positives

A desirable combination. Savvy will help steady to take a few calculated risks as long as the supporting evidence is there. Savvy's confidence will rub off on steady, enabling steady to feel secure while savvy boosts the bank account.

Savvy + timid

Pitfalls

Timid may try to reject savvy's suggestions for any kind of change. Timid will need lots of time to digest savvy's ideas and this may result in a few frustrated outbursts from savvy, who will have to work hard at providing reasons for taking risks.

Positives

Provided time is on your side, the outlook is bright. Until timid met savvy, there was little chance of financial success and the future looked grim. With savvy at their side to help with the decisions, timid should be able to reap results.

Steady + timid

Pitfalls

With a steady, cautious approach to investing, timid will find it hard to create real wealth. As steady is also naturally conservative, you both may come to the conclusion that risk is a dirty word. Your procrastination may see opportunities slide.

Positives

You both won't rush into anything risky and will favour 'safe' investments. You may even be able to predict what income you will receive for the rest of your life. There will be no financial dramas. Life will be smooth and predictable, just as you like it.

Steady + steady

Pitfalls

You may not have much of a social life as your time will be spent on research! Weighing up all the options is important to you but your procrastination may stop you from making the most of your opportunities. Growth may also be compromised.

Positives

You will really enjoy spending hours poring over books, articles and brochures, gathering your data like a bird gathers twigs. You will be comfortable with your choice of investment vehicles and be happy to wait a while to reap your rewards.

Timid + timid

Pitfalls

Unless you undergo a personality change or seek plenty of financial help, you may never be financially successful. Your worst nightmare—not enough money to fund your eventual retirement—may come true as your funds will simply not grow enough sitting in savings accounts and term deposits.

Positives

If you seek financial help from a planner who comes highly recommended and who you both trust and feel comfortable with, or by undertaking a course in investment, you may be able to push the boundaries of your comfort zone.

Of course, you may be a combination of a few financial personalities. The important point to note is that every relationship is unique and there are positives in most situations, even those with opposite financial personalities!

YOUR VALUES—WHAT IS REALLY IMPORTANT TO YOU?

Having determined your financial personality types, you need to sit down with your partner to discuss your values. Like your personality, your values help shape who you are and determine what matters most to you. They represent what you stand for and what you care most deeply about.

Funnily enough, couples often pass over a discussion on values and go straight to goal-setting. Yet, without a clear understanding of your partner's values, you will be unable to fulfil and maintain your life goals. Values such as security, emotional support, fun, fidelity, trust, health and spiritual growth can be all key aspects of your expectations about your relationship.

All too often, people fail to align their goals with their values. The result is that they may end up disappointed with their lot in life. Take Katrina, who never discussed her life values with her partner, James. She worked and worked to accumulate as many possessions as she could: a big house, flash cars and expensive clothes. Her values were security, comfort, stability and wealth.

Unfortunately for Katrina, James' values were about spiritual growth, emotional support and enjoying life. The partnership hit a rocky patch when Katrina turned 40 and realised that her and James' values—and therefore their goals—were entirely different. Sure, she had accumulated wealth, but it was at the expense of their relationship. She had spent so much time away from him that they had drifted apart.

YOUR DREAMS

You may have a dream to sail around the world or sing in a rock band. You may want three children quickly while your partner secretly wants none. Don't be afraid to share your dreams and aspirations, as they will undoubtedly have an effect on what goals you set together as a couple.

I considered friends of mine had the ideal partnership. They were paying off a beautiful apartment, both had great jobs and they were always on the social scene. Little did I know that beneath it all brewed a huge problem: he was originally from the country and longed to return, while she was a city girl.

She didn't realise that he was so serious about his dream and he thought that he could somehow change her mind. Eventually they split up, as they hadn't taken the time at the beginning of their relationship to discuss their dreams and life goals and agree on them—or, at the very least, make a few compromises.

YOUR ATTITUDES

Your background, upbringing and life experiences will all have a direct effect on your attitude to money. Sigmund Freud, for many the father of psychoanalysis, even went so far as to suggest that attitudes to spending and saving money are formed during early childhood toilet training!

Family history plays a big part in developing attitudes to finances. However, it is common for two siblings to have completely different approaches. Remember your sister or brother who always had money in the bank while you had none? The same pocket money was given to both of you but somehow one managed to save and the other didn't. So, while your family life is important, your personality and attitude to life have just as much influence.

You will notice that successful people have a distinctly positive attitude towards money. This may not have anything to do with how much they earn. Well-paid people may have an attitude to money that constantly keeps them poor while others with modest incomes may have substantial savings or investment portfolios.

For couples, finding out more about each other's attitude to money can help you understand how to align your spending and saving habits. Here are some tips to remember when discussing this essential subject:

- No single person's attitude is the right one.
- Respect a partner's feelings when discussing attitudes—try not to be judgemental about spending habits.

Values	Short-term goals	Long-term goals
Security	Start a savings plan of $200 a month	Net worth of $1 million by the age of 65
Freedom	Increase monthly mortgage payment to fortnightly	Pay off mortgage in ten years
Spirituality	Enrol in a yoga course	A trip to India in five years
Fun	Organise a holiday to Queensland in October	An overseas trip every two years

3 Act now

Don't dally. By acting sooner rather than later, you are more likely to make your goals a reality. That doesn't mean you should rush out and put a deposit down on a home next month. Just start to do your research so that you are taking steps to make your goals come true.

If you want to buy that holiday home, search the Internet for details of properties for sale. If your goal is a holiday, contact a travel agent and buy a travel guide on the region so you can read up on the history, culture and best time to visit. If you want to pay off that credit card, start making sacrifices now. Cut back on expenses such as dining out, dry-cleaning and takeaway food.

4 Seek help

People who are achievers usually recognise their own strengths and don't hesitate to enlist the help of others with greater expertise. So don't sit back and wait for your goals to happen. Take action together. Ask friends and families for help then move further afield, do some research and find the people you will need to know to help you meet your objectives. That may mean tracking down a qualified financial planner or someone who is successful in the same line of work and will therefore have plenty of ideas to help you get where you want to be. If you are keen to set up a small business, do a course and talk to experts who can give you guidance.

5 An accurate costing

Knowing how much your goals are going to cost will help you to set a budget so that you can work out how much to put aside each week. An accurate costing may also disclose that some of your goals are unrealistic. But don't be dismayed. All you may need is some tweaking of your plan.

Maybe you could rent a holiday home rather than buy one—or buy something smaller. Perhaps you could take a holiday at home rather than overseas or go for three weeks rather than four. And that debt you are keen to demolish may take eighteen months rather than twelve months to pay off.

Keep monitoring your progress. Are you hitting your targets? Have you had some unexpected bills? If so, just realign your goals to accommodate your changes in circumstances and keep moving ahead.

HOW MANY GOALS AT ONE TIME?

It is best to have two to three goals only on your plate at once. Try to assign dates and the steps required to achieve them. A simple chart, detailing who is responsible for what and when, is often handy to put on your fridge door (see Figure 2.1).

Figure 2.1 Responsibility chart

Goal: ______________________________ Short/medium-term

Completion date: ______________________________

What do you need?: ______________________________

What needs to be done?	Who is going to do it?	When is it due?
________	________	________
________	________	________
________	________	________
________	________	________

Knowing your financial personality types and discussing values, dreams, attitudes and goals can be extremely liberating for many couples. It can make the road ahead clear and will help draw you closer together. And just think how much more you will learn about your partner along the way!

3

Get help to build wealth

Myth: We can't afford a financial adviser.
Fact: There are advisers to suit most budgets.

A doctor looks after your personal health, a dentist your teeth and a solicitor your legal needs. But who cares for your financial well-being? Once you have sat down together to discuss your financial objectives, it is time to consider the merits of a financial adviser who can chart a course to help you achieve your goals—whether that's buying a home, saving for your children's education, planning for retirement or simply deciding on the smartest ways to capitalise on your hard-earned income.

A qualified, experienced financial adviser can help you to develop a sound financial program, as well as assist with informed decisions on how to make the most of your money, understand investment principles such as risk and return and choose products to suit your requirements.

There are certain times in almost everyone's life when it definitely pays to see a financial adviser. You may have built up a nest egg; you may have received a lump sum from a redundancy or inheritance; you may have experienced a change in your personal circumstances, such as retirement; or as a couple you may simply want to plan for your future together.

In these instances, it makes sense to seek help from an experienced professional. This is particularly important when you are starting out life together as a couple. If you plan properly, your future will be all the more secure.

Along with an accredited financial planner, it's also a good idea to have an accountant as part of your finance team as they can help to streamline your affairs and make the most of the tax system.

If you each already have a planner and an accountant, you have to decide whether to maintain these separate relationships, dump yours in favour of theirs, or start afresh with a new team. This will apply to other professional relationships such as solicitors and stockbrokers. Rationalising your financial affairs will keep costs down, but you both have to be convinced that your needs are given equal priority.

Of course, not everyone needs a financial adviser. Some people have the time to educate themselves and make their own financial decisions. But be cautious, as this can be compared with doing your own accounting or diagnosing your own health. It's a task often best left to the experts.

There are certain situations where creating a plan with a financial adviser is not necessary. For example, if you have sold your house and want to park your funds for only a short time—say, six months to a year—a cash-management account offering a higher interest rate than a standard bank account may be a simple solution.

If you just want to buy shares, you can easily contact a stockbroker or make use of an online discount broker. The stock exchanges in Australia can refer you to licensed stockbrokers. Or you may wish to buy units in a managed fund and already have a fund manager in mind. In this case, you can deal directly with the institution or with a licensed broker.

FINDING THE RIGHT ADVISER

Where do you find an adviser you can trust who will offer independent assistance? Where do you find one who will take a holistic approach to your personal and financial situation and who will understand your comfort level for risk? And where do you find one who will suit your budget, will listen to both of you and not just the more vocal person in the relationship, and explain the financial services industry in plain English?

A good place to start is by asking friends and colleagues for their recommendations. Quiz them about the strengths and weaknesses of their own advisers. Find out how much they charge. Is it a flat fee? Commission-based? An hourly rate? Or a percentage of your investment funds?

Some fund managers and financial institutions provide a free service often available on their Websites referring you to suitable advisers in your area. Your accountant may also be able to recommend an adviser.

Or you can contact the Financial Planning Association (FPA) of Australia on 1800 626 393 or look on the Internet at www.fpa.asn.au. The FPA's Website offers several ways to help select an adviser, including a referral service by region based on your needs whether they involve wealth creation or retirement planning. There is also a search option by company or individual surname.

Narrow your selection down to three advisers, just as you would if you were organising quotes for home renovations or repairs. Ask each to send you a copy of their advisory services guide, which will tell you whether they hold a licence from the Australian Securities and Investments Commission and whether they are an authorised representative. If not, wipe them off your shortlist.

The advisory services guide will also disclose the type of services offered by the advisers, how they are paid, whether they earn commissions on products you buy from them or whether they are linked to a bank or investment company, and how they deal with complaints. You can use this guide to compare products and services. For example, some may not be able to buy shares for you while others can organise to buy on your behalf.

You also need to find out just how much experience and expertise they have in the areas that interest you. For example, some advisers may specialise in tax advice while others focus more on managed funds; some may suit high-income earners while others are more suited to investors getting started. Find out about the type of research they can access as well as their own professional qualifications.

HOW TO INTERVIEW AN ADVISER

Before making an appointment, visit the above-mentioned FPA Website and click on frequently asked questions. Or read the FPA's free booklet, *Don't Kiss Your Money Goodbye*. Full of sound advice on choosing a financial adviser, it also has a handy list of questions to ask. These include: What kind of clients does the financial adviser see? Are they older or younger? What kind of products does the adviser know most about? How do they do their research?

When interviewing a potential adviser, you need to be aware of your thoughts and emotions. Is the adviser on the same wave-length as you? Do you feel the adviser is directing all their answers to your partner and ignoring you? If so, you may need to look elsewhere. Can you imagine an ongoing financial relationship with this person? Will they act in the best interests of both of you and not just pursue what the dominant partner wants?

After the interview, discuss your feelings openly with your partner—remember, you both need to be actively involved with any decisions you are making about money. It's a bit like establishing a rapport with a doctor. You need to have confidence in their ability to listen to what you are saying and to look after your long-term needs. This can really be put to the test when markets are fluctuating.

Tell your adviser up front if there are particular investments such as managed funds or shares in which you want to invest. Ask if there will be regular check-ups to keep your financial health in optimum shape. You'll also need to know how accessible your advisers are. Do they have a large number of clients? Do they have the time to cater to your needs? Will they be available when you call or will you have to wait days to hear from them?

You should be confident that your chosen adviser will cater for your whole life cycle by preparing a plan that takes into account your needs now and in the future.

WHAT'S IT GOING TO COST?

Some financial advisers may not charge for a first appointment. Some will have a one-off fee to prepare a financial plan. They may be commission-based or charge an hourly rate, a flat fee or take a percentage of your investment funds. Make sure you are clear about all the costs involved, including commissions, and find out whether there are any limitations on what your adviser can offer you in terms of advice.

The following is a rough guide on what you can expect to pay, according to the FPA booklet *Don't Kiss Your Money Goodbye*. Provided your finances are fairly straightforward, if you were to invest about $100 000, it may cost between $1500 and $2500 (or between 1.5–2.5 per cent commission, or $15 to $25 for every $1000 you invest) for a standard range of products. Fees for service can range anywhere from about $100 an hour to $400 an hour. Expect to pay about $200 an hour if you are paying only for the time spent and no commissions.

Once you are armed with all of the above, it's up to you to decide. Remember that making up your mind on the basis of fees alone can turn out to be a false economy. Often, it should come down to which adviser you both feel most comfortable with.

WHAT DO YOU TAKE WITH YOU?

When meeting an adviser to develop a plan, make sure you have thought carefully about your ambitions and have discussed them together. Many couples find it quite embarrassing when they share their life goals in front of an adviser—especially if it's the first time their partner has heard about them!

Friends of mine recently went to see an adviser to get their financial affairs sorted out. They had just bought their first home and had two young children. When the adviser started asking questions about Sue going back to work, she replied: 'I've no plans to return to the workforce until the children have left school.' Her husband, Tim, was aghast. This was the first he'd heard of it. He had wrongly assumed that she would return to work full time when the children *started* school, not when they'd finished! The rest of the interview was tense and they drove home in silence.

Your financial adviser may ask about:

- where you want to be financially in five or ten years;
- whether you are planning to have children;
- whether you are saving for a home, planning to move or renovate an existing property, or intending to buy an investment property or a holiday home;
- whether you are planning to fund your children's education;
- the type of holidays you enjoy;
- whether you need a new car;
- your tolerance to risk;
- your debts;
- your retirement plans;
- how much you think you need to live on;
- how much you can afford to save.

Take along as many financial details as possible, such as past tax returns, insurance commitments, superannuation fund statements, children's education costs and details of savings and investments to get the most out of that first meeting. Make a list of your assets and liabilities and work out your living expenses, saving capabilities and lifestyle needs. The more information you provide, the more likely an adviser will be to provide the right advice.

A good financial plan should:

- detail your financial position and outline your short- and long-term goals;
- take into account your preferences for investment vehicles or institutions;
- detail how each recommendation will help achieve your goals;
- recommend which investments to make and which, if any, should be sold;
- clearly outline all costs, including management fees from external parties;

- discuss any risks and how you should deal with them;
- provide a clear understanding about what commissions and/or benefits your financial adviser may receive as a result of the recommendations.

HOW MUCH RISK IS TOLERABLE?

The question of risk should be discussed at length with your partner before seeing your financial adviser. Your money personalities will come into play here: thrillseeker will have a high tolerance to risk while steady and timid will be more cautious. Depending on the couple, there are many different interpretations of what constitutes risk. Make sure your adviser provides examples of low-, medium- and high-risk investments so that you have a clear understanding of the implications of each type.

Most investors will have periods when they make money and times when they lose money. Talk to your adviser about your tolerance level. If you are a younger couple, you may wish to go for higher growth—and higher risk—investments. If you are nearing retirement, you may want to reduce your risk by opting for medium-growth products. Remember, successful investors will experience downturns but will ride them out if they are comfortable with their initial investment decisions.

BE DEMANDING

Make sure you both understand what is being offered by your financial adviser and take the time to think carefully about investment decisions after your meeting. Investment jargon can be confusing even for seasoned investors. If your adviser recommends managed funds, be clear about the asset class and about past and present investment performance. Does the fund specialise in Australian shares or does it invest across a range of classes such as domestic shares and property?

Also, find out how often you will need to see your adviser. Will once a year be sufficient or will you need to be supervised more closely? And don't be afraid to question the adviser's recommendations when markets are volatile. This can be the most crucial element in selecting an adviser and can separate the best from the not so good.

KEEP AN EYE ON YOUR PLAN

You should be looking at your plan with your adviser at least once every twelve months. It is important to check for the following things:

- Are you both happy with the advice being given?
- Are you comfortable with the investments?
- Have you achieved some of your goals?
- Have your goals changed?
- Have your circumstances changed (e.g. marriage, children)?
- Is the plan providing you with the right level of income?
- Has your attitude to risk changed?
- Do you want to add anything to your plan?

If your circumstances have changed, you may need to review your plan. Assess your new goals and organise another appointment. Your adviser may also feel the need to change some of the investments. Ask how much this will cost, particularly if the recommendation is to make new investments or switch existing ones around.

WHEN TO CHANGE ADVISERS

If your reason for wanting to switch financial advisers is because you haven't made a positive return in six months, you may be a little over-optimistic! There are few investors who have made their fortunes overnight. Remember, a good financial plan may not show positive returns for some time, especially if you are investing in the sharemarket. A friend may rave about their new planner, but the grass is not always greener on the other side of the fence.

However, if you feel that your plan has unnecessary risk, is not meeting your goals or you do not feel comfortable with your adviser, it may be time for a change. If so, follow your gut instincts, do your research again and and make your selection carefully.

Once all your homework is done, you'll find out that even a little planning can go a long way.

Tips for finding a financial adviser

1 Deal only with a licensed advisory business.
2 Choose an adviser with the strongest qualifications, experience and integrity.
3 Ask questions until you really understand the system.
4 If you feel uneasy, it's fine to walk away.
5 Make sure your financial plan suits your needs and personality.
6 When you work out a good plan, stick to it.
7 Keep all your paperwork.

Source: Financial Planning Association of Australia Ltd and Australian Securities and Investments Commission, *Don't Kiss Your Money Goodbye*, 2002.

Questions to ask an adviser

- What licences do you and your firm hold?
- What is your role within the firm and who owns it?
- What are your qualifications and how will they enable you to provide us with good service?
- How long have you been involved in financial planning?
- What practical and professional experience do you have in giving advice?
- What types of fees do you charge for: an initial consultation; a portfolio; an annual or regular review; and amending a portfolio?
- Will you or your firm receive a fee or any other incentive payment from the investments that we make?
- How do you select the investments you recommend and how will you determine what will be suitable for us?
- Do you provide a written financial report and what information will it contain?
- What types of services are we entitled to receive if we become clients?
- Can you provide the names of existing clients prepared to endorse your firm?

Resist the urge to splurge

Hanna and Peter were a one-income family in their mid-thirties when Hanna's only surviving relative passed away, leaving them a $50 000 inheritance. Her first thought was to plan a luxury overseas holiday with their two children. Her next idea was to buy a new car and renovate their small two-bedroom home. Perhaps they could upgrade the family computer, too.

After a few weeks in which she had spent the money many times over in her mind, Hanna realised she needed a helping hand. Peter suggested they seek the services of a financial adviser.

Financial planner Rob Pedersen, of Matrix Planning Solutions, says Hanna and Peter are typical of so many people who come into money unexpectedly. Their first thoughts are to splurge on something expensive to make them feel good. But this is such a short-term vision. By taking a longer term view, they can actually set themselves up so that they can afford some of the things they desire and make their daily lives seem less of a grind.

During their first meeting, Rob helped them with a strategy to free up some income and reduce their burden of debt. He suggested that their key priority should be to eliminate their credit card debt, which had an annual interest rate of 15 per cent. That would leave them with $47 500 to reduce their mortgage.

The repayments on their $150 000 home loan over a twenty-year term with an interest rate of 6.5 per cent were $1118 a month. By paying $47 500 off the loan, the repayments would fall to $764 a month, saving them $354 a month.

Hanna and Peter then were given several options. They could reinvest the $354 a month into a managed fund and start to build up a portfolio. Once they reached a target of $10 000, they could consider taking out a loan of $20 000 to negatively gear the investment. The interest component on the $20 000 would be tax deductible.

Or, further down the track, they could approach an institution to reborrow the $47 500 they paid off their mortgage and invest that in a managed fund. The interest component on the $47 500 would then become a tax deduction too because they had borrowed money from the bank to reinvest in an income-producing vehicle.

Of course, both gearing strategies also involved some risks. However, if Hanna and Peter had decided to put their $50 000 inheritance straight into a managed fund without paying a cent off their mortgage, there would have been few tax advantages. They decided on the first option.

Rob also suggested that, once they had paid off their credit card debt and reduced their mortgage with the balance of the inheritance, they should save a portion of the $354 for the first few months to take a decent holiday. They should regard this as a bonus for taking the time to make the best use of their windfall.

Setting goals

Jo and Tim weren't as lucky as Hanna and Peter and were virtually starting from scratch. The Perth couple were both aged in their early thirties, with a combined income of $80 000. They hoped to start a family in the next few years. Unlike many couples in their situation, the only debt they had was a sports car bought on a whim. Their short-term goals were to purchase an apartment within the next two years, have an overseas holiday every four years and be able to dine out once a week. Financial planner Marisa Broome, principal of wealthadvice.com, recommended the couple visit a planner to draw up a budget so they would know where they were spending their funds. Then they would need to set short-, medium- and long-term savings goals. In this case, the short-term goal was the apartment, the medium-term one the overseas holiday every four years, and the long-term goal some shares and their superannuation.

Marisa explained:

> These goals require different ways of saving. Short-term funds should be in a high yielding and accessible account like a cash management trust or a bonus saver, medium could be invested in a conservatively managed share fund like a capital stable fund or even a listed property trust, long term means they have the time frame to see out volatility, so they could have some exposure to international and Australian shares.
>
> I would suggest that, to meet their goals more quickly, they try living off one income and paying off the car as soon as possible. It would be foolish to tell them to sell it,

> as financial planning is about meeting lifestyle and financial goals, not compromising one for the other—especially with younger clients. Once the car is paid out, the savings could be directed to the deposit for a property. They will need at least 20 per cent deposit plus stamp duty and costs.
>
> As property is expensive to buy and sell, we often advise clients to think about their medium-term lifestyle before buying. For Jo and Tim, who are keen to start a family, it would make more financial sense to save for an extra few years to buy a house rather than an apartment to minimise all the costs associated with buying and selling a second time.

As they were first-home buyers, Jo and Tim would be eligible for any first-home buyers assistance packages available from the federal government. While saving for the house, the overseas holiday could be put on hold or downgraded to a cheaper destination. Dining out once a week should not be an issue.

They should also not forget their long-term goals and ensure that their superannuation is invested correctly and working well for them.

4

Taking control of debt

Myth: We'll never be financially successful because we can't see past our debts.
Fact: You have a choice about how you spend your money—it's all about taking control.

Levels of personal debt have climbed to an all-time high as our need-it-now society spends rather than saves. Unlike the parents and grandparents of the baby boomers, who rarely had the opportunity to buy goods unless they paid cash, the current social trend is more about instant gratification, an obsession with plastic and an almost fearless disregard for debt.

Couples may have two, three or even four credit cards exceeding their hefty limits, along with a mighty mortgage and a car loan biting deeply into hard-earned pay packets. Yet, in this consumer-conscious world, the decision to buy goods—from a wide-screen television to the latest sofa—is often made on the spur of the moment. Sums are not done, budgets are rarely consulted and interest rates barely register as the plastic is pushed to the limit and beyond.

It is easy to blame this spending regime on credit cards and the seductive and flattering offers by banks of incentives such as gold cards and increased credit limits. But it's up to you and your partner to take control of your finances. No one else will do it.

Of course, you and your partner's financial personalities will be a force in how money is spent. Thrillseeker types may thrive on living on the edge, taking risks and juggling debt. But if the other partner is the steady type, this may be enough to drive you to the Family Law Court.

Serious debt can place a big strain on a relationship, so it is important to agree early on how much debt you can tolerate. You also need to do a budget and control your spending. And yes, it's that easy.

Of course, debt is not always of your own making. In an era where retrenchments are all too common, it is easy to see how couples may find it difficult to make ends meet. Even a small rise in mortgage interest rates can send some spiralling into debt, particularly if the budget is stretched too tight already. And with rising rates of divorce and separation, couples can suddenly become single parents with debt a constant companion.

DEBT CAN RUIN YOUR HEALTH

Apart from all the obvious financial implications, debt may have an adverse impact on your physical well-being. Do you find yourself worrying constantly about credit card liabilities? Are you consumed with fear that you may have to sell your car in order to finance your rent or home loan? Is it becoming harder to make ends meet? Are there endless arguments about the state of your finances?

If so, you need to stop reacting and take action because your debts may be damaging your health and your relationship. Conditions such as insomnia, stress-related eczema or digestive upsets may be a surefire sign that excessive worry is taking its toll.

You can take some comfort in the fact that you are not alone. In Australia, household debt has soared from $150 billion to $357 billion in a decade, leaving an increasing number of people with few options but to draw on whatever savings they have. While retail therapy may make you feel better in the short term, it may only add to your woes in the long run. Remember, problems with debt don't have to be permanent. With careful planning, time and patience, you can end the debt cycle and start to set some serious goals for your financial future.

ARE WE REALLY IN SERIOUS DEBT?

If most of your friends share the same situation, you can be tricked into thinking that your level of debt as a couple is not a problem, even though a little voice inside tells you otherwise. My advice is to sit down together and put a tick beside any of the following points that relate to you. If one partner pays the bills and the other is oblivious to your financial plight, now is the time to be honest and confess.

- You are in the habit of impulse buying even though you know you don't have the money to pay for the goods.
- You have two or more credit cards between you maxed to the limit.
- You rely on cash advances from your credit cards to pay off your bills.
- You take a cash advance from one credit card to pay off the minimum balance of another.
- You sweat on your pay day to meet your bills.
- You are about to default on a mobile phone payment.
- You make sure you beat your partner to the letterbox to get your credit card statement.
- You never knock back an offer from the bank to increase your card limit. You are even flattered that they have made the offer!
- You are often threatened with disconnection notices for late payments.
- A store owner hands you the phone when they ring to get a credit clearance for the birthday present you planned to buy your partner.

If you have answered yes to at least three of the above, you may have a debt problem. If you have answered yes to four or more, you may have a serious problem and it could be time to seek financial help. There are many avenues of help available which are detailed later in this chapter.

HOW COUPLES GET INTO DEBT

Couples can get into debt in so many ways. It may have to do with living life to the full. Or it may be that their parents were part of the baby boomer generation whose attitude was that we are here for a good time rather than a long time.

Instead of marrying in their late teens or early twenties, many people now spend their twenties blowing whatever meagre savings they have accumulated on overseas trips, nice cars, up-to-the-minute wardrobes and entertainment. By the time they hit 30, they wonder where it has all gone!

Social researcher Hugh Mackay said:

> My research shows that, generally speaking, around about the age of 30 people are only just beginning to come out of the sense of being kids. It's all happening about ten years later than it used to. So at 30 they are saying: 'Gee, when my parents were this age they were married, had three kids, a mortgage and my Dad had a career.' I'm 30 and I've just stopped going to nightclubs!

Mackay believes that the stigma attached to debt has gone because the word 'debt' has been replaced by the more respectable term 'credit'. Unlike credit, 'debt' sounds as though you are in trouble.

Of course, some also innocently inherit debt from their partner.

SEXUALLY TRANSMITTED DEBT

Do you have a joint credit card arrangement with your partner? A home loan with a facility to withdraw what you have paid off? Have you ever been persuaded to go guarantor on a loan? To be a co-borrower?

For many couples, joint arrangements are a normal state of affairs, and often little thought is given to the risks involved as both parties happily sign on the dotted line. But what happens if the relationship sours and your partner skips town, leaving you with what has become known as sexually transmitted debt (STD)?

Take the case of Charles and Susan, who had been married for two years. He wanted to upgrade the family car but, having just lost his job, the bank was understandably reluctant to lend him the money. He asked Susan, who had held a steady job for ten years, if she would borrow $35 000 jointly with him. Since they also had a joint bank account, she didn't think twice about it.

Susan didn't read the fine print of the contract and simply scrawled her signature on the dotted line. She didn't even consider the following issues: What are my financial responsibilities if I sign this document? What is the maximum I might have to repay? What can go wrong (redundancy, injury, illness, relationship breakdown) to stop my partner from meeting the repayments? Will I be able to pay off the loan if he can't? Am I in a position to put myself at such a risk in the first place?

She naively thought she was simply vouching for her partner's good character and that agreeing to sign the document was a mere formality. She ignored the fact that, as co-borrowers, she and her partner were each responsible for the whole debt. In other words, if he didn't meet the repayments, she would be required to repay the whole amount.

Two years later, their relationship did break down. He skipped town in their new four-wheel drive and, despite every avenue—family, friends, police and private detectives—she could not locate him.

As Susan was a co-borrower on the loan, she was liable for the outstanding amount, plus the interest. He had also cleaned out their joint bank account, leaving her with a nasty case of STD.

This is a scenario witnessed regularly by services such as the Consumer Credit Legal Centre in New South Wales. Katherine Lane, a solicitor with the Centre, says:

> In these situations, women in particular are often encouraged to think co-borrowing is a formality and that nothing can go wrong. By doing that, they are encouraged to under-rate the extent of the risk, which is that either party can be pursued for the full amount and in some scenarios it is easier to pursue the female co-borrower because she is around and has a more stable employment history.

> We believe that people should not be signed up as co-borrowers unless they are going to benefit from the loan—that is, two people who genuinely want to buy a car or other item and will be using it together.

As a co-borrower, Susan probably does not have any recourse, says a spokesperson for the New South Wales Department of Fair Trading:

> She would have to argue at the Consumer Trader and Tenancy Tribunal that the circumstance of what she was doing was misrepresented and wasn't explained to her adequately by the credit provider. But if she were present at the time the application for the loan was made then it might be hard to argue that she didn't understand what she was doing.

When it comes to joint bank accounts, where either party can withdraw funds, Lane advises couples to think seriously before taking this step. Unless you feel you are in the kind of a relationship where you can trust the person not to take everything, do not have joint accounts. The same applies to credit cards where spouses may have a subsidiary card that can leave the cardholder liable for any expenditure.

Some spouses are talked into acting as guarantor on a partner's business loans, agreeing to put joint assets such as a house up as security in the event the business folds. But what they may not realise is that by going guarantor, they are undertaking to pay if the borrower cannot.

> Before you agree to be guarantor, you need to know how much is available to be borrowed, if further increases on the loan will be available, what securities are being taken by the lending institution and what is at stake if the loan is not repaid, Lane says. You also need to be aware of how well the business is going because if it does fail, you could easily lose your home. And if the relationship collapses and the spouse takes off then the remaining spouse or partner may be left with the debt.

Women in particular may feel pressured into agreeing to a joint arrangement—sometimes without understanding the extent of their liability. After all, few people like to contemplate the worst and many find it difficult to say no—especially to their loved ones.

A home loan redraw facility is another area where STD can strike. For example, if one partner has a gambling addiction and wants cash fast, he or she may resort to withdrawing the equity in their home loan.

> Today, there is not enough emphasis on the risks involved, especially on redraw facilities, Lane says. If you have a joint credit card with a limit of $5000 then the worst-case scenario is that you can use up your credit to the tune of $5000. But if you have a redraw facility with several hundred thousand dollars of equity available and the bank is not notified in time to stop the withdrawal then there is a lot at stake.

Protect yourself against STDs

- Consider separate accounts and credit cards.
- When setting up a loan in joint names, insist that both signatures be required for redrawing funds or increasing the loan.
- Review finances together regularly.
- Do your research and consider getting legal advice before going guarantor or acting as co-borrower on a loan.
- Agree to act as a guarantor only if you trust your partner implicitly and will be able to pay any costs for the duration of the loan—even if they can't (or won't).
- **Don't be coerced into anything you are not comfortable with or anything you don't fully understand.**
- Be comfortable in saying 'no'. Also consider whether you are obtaining any benefit from the transaction.

IMPULSE BUYING

A friend of mine, Mickie, is a personal fitness trainer and consequently has to be extremely disciplined in many aspects of her life. She can say no to a hamburger without blinking an eye, but when it comes to a new pair of shoes, all her self-control goes out the window.

Are you or your partner an impulse buyer? Think carefully before answering for your partner, because impulse buyers can be pretty clever at hiding their tracks!

An impulse buyer will typically shop until they drop without being able to stop. They will get a great sense of satisfaction out of the event and will often buy things they don't need.

Take Amy and Joe, who are both impulse buyers. Amy goes to a local shopping centre about once a fortnight. On the face of it, this seems perfectly normal. However, when she does go, she spends up big. She goes from one clothes shop to the next buying new fashion pieces to bolster what she believes is a boring wardrobe. When she arrives home, she may find she has bought similar items on previous sprees but justifies the new purchases as being 'slightly' different.

Joe, on the other hand, frowns at Amy's frivolous nature. He can't understand how she can be so irresponsible in spending their money. However, he forgets that whenever he goes to the hardware store he comes home with yet another power tool that he just has to have. Or the times that he disappears to the gadget shop and comes back with another device to save time, organise his diary and, of course, keep track of their finances. Let alone the new single remote control to take the place of four others at a cost of only $400. Think of all the time they will both save viewing the new plasma screen TV that he has affixed to the ceiling of their bedroom!

The scary thing is that Amy and Joe are not that unusual. So what do you do about being an impulse buyer?

The first step is to try to identify what triggers the impulse. If it is shopping centres, then set yourself a target not to visit one for three months. Ditto for hardware or gadget shops. When you do take the plunge, take cash only. That way, you will be forced to make a rational decision about what you can afford. If you have serious credit card debts because of your extravagances, hopefully you will have already cut up your cards. If not, do so immediately!

CREDIT CARDS

Most couples have at least one credit card to use for emergencies and special occasions, or just for the convenience of not having to carry around large amounts of cash. As I've mentioned earlier, some savvy and steady personality types pay off their debts in full each month to avoid being charged any fees. For those who aren't that disciplined, have you ever thought seriously about how much credit cards cost you?

Financial institutions charge interest rates of about 15–16 per cent—some more, some less—for a standard credit card. This figure is, of course, linked to interest-rate movements so that if rates rise so too do credit card charges. It means that, regardless of low or high inflation, the institutions still earn a healthy return on their lending with little risk. The most we mere mortals can hope to earn in interest in a similar period is significantly less. No wonder they are so keen to sign us up!

Interest is not the only charge on the credit card. Credit card providers have been clever in establishing fees for a number of things—first there is the annual fee that varies from $20 to $120 per annum; then there is an over-the-limit fee; as well, they charge late payment fees and cash advance interest from the time you obtain a cash advance until the entire account is paid.

Take the cash-strapped couple whose second-hand fridge died suddenly one day. They used a brand new credit card to buy a $1500 fridge, convincing each other that they would take six months only to pay it off because the interest rate was so high. But there was always another expense to meet and it actually took them almost two years to pay it off.

They could have bought a microwave with the interest they incurred! And don't forget about the annual or monthly fees charged for the privilege of using a credit card.

The general rule is that if you can't pay off your credit card debts in full each month, cut them up and don't use them. If not, they will cost you big time. If you can't survive without one, learn everything you can about the conditions on your credit card. Find out about fees, interest-free periods, late payment charges and interest rates.

STORE CARDS

Free gift wrapping, an extra year's warranty, no annual fees, twelve month interest-free credit provided you spend a certain amount, 10 per cent discounts . . . these are just some of the perks used to lure shoppers to sign up for store cards.

At first glance, they seem too good to resist. And, for the prudent shopper, store cards can offer genuine discounts and frills. But for those who are not disciplined, there are plenty of traps, with some interest rates rising to a whopping 27 per cent!

Before signing up for a store card, make sure you check the fine print carefully. Be aware of the interest rates, the costs (if any) and the benefits. Then ask yourself: do you really need another form of credit?

The idea behind such cards is to get you to do your shopping in the one store or chain. But the store in question may not always have the best prices on all goods, so not only will you pay high interest, you may also pay more for your goods than you need to.

Catherine Wolthuizen, finance policy officer with the Australian Consumers' Association, says that if you don't pay those particular loans when they are due, there may be all sorts of backtracking penalties—for example, interest charges backdating to purchase dates.

Another key issue, according to Wolthuizen, is that store cards are so easy to obtain—a concern for people who may not be able to afford them:

> They are heavily promoted, too. If people have a credit facility they should think hard about whether they want another one—particularly one with a relatively high interest rate. They should look closely to see if the reward system that comes with them suits their spending patterns and needs.
>
> Interest-free deals are also a real worry. These lines of credit are aggressively marketed to consumers and represent a real trap if people don't pay off their debt in the set period. If you are only making minimum payments, you won't pay off the debt in time and the interest-free period is often followed by rates currently as high as 27 per cent.

> The idea that you will pay off the debt in twelve months can seem quite manageable, but it may not be so easy. If you don't pay off that debt in the period and there is a 27 per cent interest rate, that will get you into trouble very quickly. Another concern is that they have some very aggressive and novel marketing to use them as revolving credit—buying more rather than ever paying off the debt.

There is another matter to consider, too: your credit rating. Every time you apply for credit, you may be listed with an organisation such as Baycorp Advantage, one of the largest sources in Australia of credit information on individuals and companies. If you actively seek credit from a number of organisations, and have a number of listings for credit, this could tell a future lender that you may be a credit risk.

MOBILE PHONES

If you are in the market for a mobile, take the checklist from Chapter 5 with you and do your sums. But remember, if you are trying to budget and your debts are getting in the way, you really need to think seriously about whether you need one or even two mobiles.

Alternatively, you can follow the example of my stepdaughter, Kristen. She was saving to go overseas but couldn't possibly go without her mobile phone. Her boyfriend had already left and they were understandably keen to stay in contact. Instead of paying the maximum if she had to phone during the day, Kristen opted for a pre-paid phone card account. This ensured that she paid for the calls before she made them and didn't rack up a huge bill—easy to do when a loved one is far away.

LIVING BEYOND YOUR MEANS

You don't really have to have everything now. You just think you do. I remember my parents telling me that when they married, their first home had no furniture, just up-turned boxes to sit on. They slowly saved up enough for a couch, fridge, bed, and so on, and proudly enjoyed each new item.

It is certainly a different story now. If you were to move in with your partner, you would probably want a house full of furniture and the latest appliances. If you didn't have the basics, you might put them on credit. And if you were feeling worn out from months of hard work, you might think nothing of borrowing money to take a well-deserved holiday.

Living beyond your means extends further than white goods and holidays. The dream of owning your own home can also stretch couples to the limit, with average household debt currently at dangerously high levels. Rather than saving up a bigger deposit or opting for a more modest home or flat, too many are prepared to plunge heavily into debt for their quota of bricks and mortar.

Living beyond your means can lead to serious debt problems. If you both compromise by taking a little longer to achieve your goals, it will be worth it in the end.

Seven ways to reduce your debt

- *Consolidate your debts.* If you have several credit card debts, consider a personal loan with a lower interest rate to cover the total amount.
- *Refer to the Money Plan* (see Appendix 1). List all your debts and how much you need to pay them off, then include them in your budget. Don't forget to cut up all your credit cards.
- *Contact your creditors.* Most will help you to find a solution, either by extending your repayments or reducing the amount you pay each time.
- *List your debts in order of importance.* Pay off the one with the highest interest rate first but still pay the minimum on the others.
- *Adjust your lifestyle.* Be a one- instead of two-car family, focus on what you spend on entertainment and set a weekly allowance.
- If you are suffering hardship and have a loan contract you may be able to *vary the contract* for reduced repayments or to add your outstanding arrears to the end of your loan. Seek assistance from the Department of Fair Trading or a financial counsellor.
- *Get help.* For those who can't get on track, there are several agencies you can turn to for help, many offering free services that

will provide strategies and solutions to help restore some normality to your life. Agencies include:
NSW: Credit Helpline, 1800 808 488; Ryde–Eastwood Financial Counselling Service, 02 9858 1377;
Victoria: Credit Helpline, 1800 803 800;
South Australia: Family and Youth Services, 08 8226 7000;
Queensland: Financial Counselling Services, 07 3257 1957 or www.fcsq.org.au;
Tasmania: Anglicare Financial Counselling Service, 03 6234 3510;
Western Australia: Department for Community Development, 08 9222 2555;
National: Lifeline: 131114.

INTEREST RATE HIKES

Most banks will factor a small rise in interest rates into your loan repayments. This is taken into account when determining whether you can afford the mortgage. However, they don't take into account what happens when interest rates soar. If you are already living on the breadline, this can topple you over the edge. The best way to avoid interest rate increases is to try to pay a little more than the maximum required. It doesn't have to be much, but it will help cushion you when interest rates move north. If they don't move, it means you will pay more off your loan faster, which can't be a bad thing.

ADDICTION PROBLEMS

An addiction problem can mean anything from drugs or alcohol through to a shoe fetish or motorcycle obsession. A gambling addiction may see a partner sneaking off to a hotel or club to play the poker machines or calling a broker incessantly to play the stockmarket.

Identifying that there really is an addiction is the hardest part. Narelle Brown, coordinator of the Ryde–Eastwood Financial Counselling Service in Sydney, says:

> The warning signs are recognisable if you choose to see them. Your partner may be offering a lot of excuses. Their secretiveness might come from having an addiction: gambling, alcohol or a spending problem.
>
> Another warning sign is you find that you aren't receiving your statements from the bank and you notice that you haven't seen a credit card bill for a while. It's those sorts of things that just don't add up.
>
> Your partner might be anxious to get to the mail box first. You might get lots of unexplained phone calls, with the caller refusing to identify themselves but wanting to speak to your partner. You might discover that your partner is only paying the minimum amount on your credit card and you thought that you had enough cash to pay for it in full. They might suggest that you need more than one credit card.

Brown says most people who seek advice from a financial counsellor have, on average, six to eight credit cards, are typically aged 25 to 45 and have varied incomes. In fact, it is often the clients who appear to be quite wealthy who have real trouble dealing with spiralling debt, as they are more able to access credit.

If you suspect your partner has a gambling or addiction problem, don't ignore it. Tackling the issue either directly with your partner or by seeking financial counselling may be the single most important thing you ever do for your relationship.

A PARTNER'S DEBTS

There seems to be a cloud of mystery surrounding this issue. Of course, when you are in love, you can sometimes choose to view partners and their faults in a rosy light. But when it comes to dealing with a partner's debts, don't be fooled. Taking on such debts is a noble gesture if you can afford it. However, partners will never learn that they are responsible for their own actions if you continually bail them out. Brown says:

> We get a lot of people coming in for help who are really worried that they are going to be up for their partner's debts. This is not the case. They worry that once they have moved in together they will suddenly have all these debts to pay. The fact is that the new partner is not liable for any debts unless he or she is a joint or co-borrower.

Brown cites a recent case where a young woman about to move in with her boyfriend came to her office. Her new partner had significant debts and she was concerned about how she was going to pay her own debts, the rent and food and his debts as well. Brown asked: 'Why do you feel so responsible for those debts?' The young woman replied: 'We are a couple now so everything is joined together.'

Thankfully, Brown set her straight and explained that being a couple didn't necessarily mean that everything was joined. So they weighed up her partner's options for dealing with his debts. Then they discussed whether he could afford to live with her, given the costs of the house, electricity, food, and so on. What was he doing with his money that meant he couldn't pay his debts? It might be that he needed to deal with his financial situation before they could actually live together.

It was a big step for the young woman to raise the matter with her boyfriend, so Brown gave her some tips. In the end, she told her partner that she didn't know how they were going to cope financially and she didn't think living together would work. Understandably, her partner was upset and wanted to know why. But, because she had already sought financial counselling, she convinced him to go along as well. Once he had done that, she promised to reconsider the offer of cohabitating.

Being in debt need not last forever. There is plenty of help available, but you have to want to change your lifestyle and control your spending. Ultimately, getting out of debt is an emotional and financial decision that can change your life.

CHRISTMAS—KEEP IT JOLLY

As Christmas rolls around, there is nothing like a big credit card statement to take the joy out of the season. Yuletide cheer can so easily turn to despair if you blow your budget on expensive gifts and over-indulge through impulse buying.

If you're not careful, you may find you both spend most of the next year trying to make a dent in the debt. By the time next Christmas rolls around, you may still be in no shape to buy even a bon bon.

If you haven't been putting money aside for presents, it's never too too late to start. Even an extra $20 a week can make all the difference. Here are some other strategies to ensure the Christmas season is a jolly one:

- Before embarking on your Christmas spree, draw up a budget together and stick to it. Don't forget to allow for everyday expenses too.
- Make a list of presents to help prevent you from impulse buying. That way you won't spend money on unnecessary gifts.
- Leave your plastic at home and rely on cash to make any purchases. It will help you to keep track of how much you are spending and will ensure there won't be any unpleasant surprises when you open your January credit card statement!
- Try not to get too pressured by advertising. Focus on gifts that are appropriate and affordable.
- Be realistic when you set a limit on gifts. Most people, including children, enjoy a well thought out, reasonably priced gift in preference to something expensive that they will never use.
- Suggest to your family that everyone buy just one gift per family member. You simply pull out a name from a hat and buy a gift for that one person. This is a wonderful way for big families to save money at Christmas. You can set a limit of, say, $25 per gift and spend time researching what that person really needs.
- If you buy gifts for friends, chat to them about changing this policy. You can still celebrate but without the pressure of having to buy presents. Suggest catching up over a drink, a meal or a picnic.
- To save money, consider making your own presents, cards, decorations, gift tags and wrapping paper.
- When buying gifts, ask the store about its refund policy.
- And a tip for next year . . . at the January sales, stock up on appropriate gifts for next Christmas and start putting aside extra funds from February onwards to ease that end-of-year burden.

BANKRUPTCY DILEMMA

If you or your partner can't meet your financial commitments and you have the sheriff knocking at your door, you may be forced to declare yourself bankrupt. There is no minimum level of borrowings if the individual opts for bankruptcy. But if you owe creditors more than $2000, then they can declare you bankrupt.

This may be a welcome relief to some couples who have been living with the burden of their debts. But it should not be taken lightly because there are serious consequences. For example, take the case of Monique and Brad. Their home was in joint names so the insolvency trustee insisted on selling the home to recoup Monique's debts from her small business failure. Brad, however, received his portion of the equity after the sale of the home. If the home had been in his name, they would have needed to prove to the trustee that Monique had not contributed funds to improve the value of the home. If the home had been in her name only, the equity would have been used to pay creditors.

Monique also had a car worth $20 000 which the insolvency trustee sold. Bankrupts are allowed to have a car up to the value of $5500 so she received $5500 from the sale of her car and the rest went to creditors.

While the harassment stopped and her debts were wiped, Monique and Brad were forced to rent a home. Monique was unable to travel overseas without the permission of the trustee, she was bankrupt for the required three years and the bankruptcy was noted on her credit reference report for seven years, making it difficult to obtain a loan or even rent a fridge.

Monique took advantage of the free financial counselling services provided by the government to help her find the best outcome. I suggest you do the same if you are in this position. For more details on bankruptcy, visit the Insolvency Trustee Service of Australia at www.itsa.gov.au

The next chapter on budgeting should help you to get your finances on track.

5

The blueprint for budgeting

Myth: A budget is for couples on low incomes and means years of suffering and sacrifice.

Fact: Budgeting is the cornerstone of saving and will help you to take control of your finances, ensuring a richer life and relationship.

If you find the idea of doing a budget about as much fun as sitting in a traffic jam, you're not alone. When most couples think about budgeting, they usually have bleak visions of deprivation, settling for Vegemite rather than smoked salmon sandwiches at lunchtime.

It need not be that way. The aim of a budget is not to stop you doing the things you enjoy because you can't afford them. Quite the opposite. A budget can actually free up spare cash so that you'll know exactly what you can afford—and when. It is one of the best planning tools at your disposal and can set you on the path to wealth creation.

Budgeting is really all about taking control of your money and making it work for you. Once you make a commitment to a budget and stick to it, you will know where your money is going. You will develop a savings habit so you can focus on achieving long- and short-term goals.

In Chapter 1, I mentioned how a relationship is similar to a business. It should be run along the same lines, with regular health checks to see what shape it is in and whether or not it needs an overhaul or maybe a bit more communication.

All sound businesses have budgets, and their growth depends on how well they manage their budgeting and how effective it is in helping them to reach their targets—for example, a 20 per cent profit margin. A relationship is no different. If you are keen to get ahead, save for a home, pay off your mortgage and car loans, wipe out credit card debt and have enough in the kitty for holidays and superannuation, you need to work together on a budget now.

WHEN IT'S TIME FOR A BUDGET

Certain events in your life will or should be a trigger to draw up a budget:

- moving in together;
- marriage;
- the birth of a child;
- saving for a home/car/investment property;
- a change in employment;
- a pay rise;
- the new year or new financial year;
- unemployment;
- divorce;
- retirement.

WHERE DOES OUR MONEY GO?

Many couples are clueless about where their money goes each week. They have no idea about either how much they are spending or how much they are saving.

Take the case of Alex and Samantha, both aged in their mid-thirties. They have been together for ten years yet they can not tell you how much they live off each week. They each have separate accounts, from which they draw out varying amounts each week to cover their expenses. They put most of their purchases on credit cards which they pay off in full each month. While that is admirable, they rarely have any spare cash for holidays with their two children, they pay the minimum off their home loan and their superannuation is well below the norm.

Some weeks Alex will withdraw $300 and five days later he will be left with just $10 and have no idea what happened to the other $290. He has kept no receipts and has simply dug into his wallet whenever he felt like it. Sound familiar? 'Sometimes I feel like I am driving a car without any brakes,' he says. 'I just keep powering through money without putting any stops on it and I never think about where it is going or what I could be doing with it.'

Deep down, Alex and Samantha know they are putting off the inevitable day when they will have to draw up a budget so they can attain some of their goals and address their debt levels.

If, like Alex and Samantha, you have taken the biggest step of all—to commit to a partner for life and start a family—you should be able to make the next move and commit to a sensible budget to enhance your relationship and your lifestyle—yes, your lifestyle! Sure, you may have to cut back on some of life's little luxuries for a while, but the best budgets are flexible enough to factor in some fun money—and those smoked salmon sandwiches.

All that is required is a small amount of time to sit down together and work through your comings and goings. You will need to be ruthlessly honest about your spending habits because this is not the time to go into denial.

SPEND ONE INCOME, SAVE THE OTHER

Some couples struggle to live off two incomes. But, if it is feasible, living on one income and saving the other is a smart way to reach your goals faster. Chances are that at some stage one of you will need time off—through pregnancy, because of illness, to study or to find a job. Then what happens? Life will seem like extra hard work if you have been living on two incomes then all of a sudden you are left to juggle just the one salary. Could you cope? How would you pay the bills, the mortgage, the car loan, the school fees? Chapter 6 covers this in more detail.

On the other hand, if you have been used to living off one income and saving the other, if and when one partner does take time out all you will have to do is stop payments to your savings account, not to your home loan provider. So take a few minutes to think about whether and how you could manage on one income then base your budget around that income. If you have separate accounts, you can still have funds transferred into your accounts via a direct debit arrangement.

As well as a cushion for when the going gets tough, living on one income will help to make your dreams a reality as you will be investing the other income instead of spending it.

If, for whatever reason, saving one income and living off the other doesn't work for you, aim for each of you to save between 10 and 15 per cent of your incomes. Again, this will depend on your earning and saving capacity and also on your expenses.

HOW TO DRAW UP A BUDGET

It is up to you to decide how formal your budget will be. It can be as simple as a handwritten back-of-an-envelope list of income and expenses or as complicated as a computer spreadsheet.

You can invest in specialised budgeting software, you can kickstart your new budget-conscious lifestyle by using free Internet software provided by the main banks on their Websites or you can use the Money Plan in Chapter 6. The software allows you to key in your expenses and then does the calculations for you. By making some simple adjustments to the figures, you can see what you might achieve. It's all in your hands.

Remember, budgeting is a fairly simple concept: the amount you spend should always be less than the amount that's coming in. But somehow, most of us find the amount that goes out is always harder to manage. If you're genuinely unclear about where all your money goes, it's a good idea to keep a daily diary of your expenses for a month. Don't forget to record absolutely everything. The smallest items, such as coffee and newspapers, all add up.

So either sit down at your computer together or take out a pen and paper. Your personal budget planner should be drawn up into in three main sections—income, fixed expenses and controllable expenses—with room for each month of the year.

If you are paid fortnightly or weekly, you may prefer to record everything on that basis. This will make it easy for you to manage your cashflow and you will then know when to put aside extra cash to pay your bills. You should include your income from all sources, including annual bonuses, tax refunds and investment earnings. When listing your income, it is better to under-estimate than over-estimate so that anything over the predicted amount is a bonus. So only include overtime and allowances you're certain of receiving.

The next step is to record your fixed expenses, such as mortgage, rent, child care, car registration, utilities or medical insurance, and the dates on which they are paid.

Then list your controllable expenses. Don't forget all those 'hidden' expenses, such as haircare and your mobile phone bill. Controllable expenses are those where you have some leeway, hopefully without causing drastic changes to your lifestyle. Don't worry if you don't get everything down. You're bound to miss out on obvious items at your first attempt but as time goes by you will get all the details down.

Once it's all in black and white, you can look a bit more closely at what you are spending your money on and why. This will help you to establish priorities and set realistic savings goals.

Now it's time for the moment of reckoning. Add up each column then deduct your total expenses from your total income. If your income is greater than your expenses, you're in good shape. If not, you are living beyond your means and need to take a serious look at your budget.

While you can't do much about fixed expenses such as child care, home loans and insurance payments, it's controllable expenses such as entertainment, clothing, babysitting, dry cleaning, takeaway food and so on which you may be able to cut back in some way. Trim your controllable expenses and you may be pleasantly surprised by how much you have left to save and invest.

Now and then, evaluate your plan and make adjustments where necessary. If interest rates rise, you may need to alter certain categories and you may have to consider strategies such as reducing your home loan payments. If you receive a windfall or a pay rise, then once again go back to your original figures and make the necessary changes.

If you are finding your budget is not working, follow these golden rules:

- *Be flexible.* Like a rigid diet, an inflexible budget will not work unless you have breathing space. If you like eating out or going to live shows, factor this under the heading of fun money. But don't allow so much flexibility that it affects your saving and investment potential.
- *Be realistic.* You have to ensure that you have set aside enough to pay all your bills so you do not eat into your savings.
- *Set goals.* Remember Chapter 2 about goal-setting and values? To set a proper budget, you need a clear idea of both. Otherwise, you will have no idea what you are saving for.
- *Reward yourselves.* When you reach certain milestones, celebrate with a special night out or whatever takes your fancy.

And don't be frightened to create a new budget.

HOW TO SAVE AN EXTRA $300 A MONTH

With a little planning, it may be easier than you think to put something extra aside, even up to $300 at a time. Here are some surefire ways to get started. Your wallet should be the big winner.

My friend, Rosie and her partner, Steve, tried this exercise and found they could easily save about $300 a month with some minor sacrifices such as one cappuccino a day rather than two (they slept better, too); takeaway meals twice rather than five times a fortnight; eating out once rather than twice a month at a medium-priced restaurant; cutting their intake of alcohol; going to the movies on discount days rather than weekends; and cutting the cost of their fitness regimes. Rosie was pleasantly surprised:

The key was in the planning. We usually spent about $30 on takeaway each time so cutting that back to twice a fortnight saved us $90 a month alone. We usually ate out twice a month, costing us about $80 a time. By only dining out once a month, there's an extra $80.

By eating fewer takeaway meals, we also improved our diet, lowered our cholesterol and saved more money by not wasting the food we had bought at the supermarket. We also cut back on wine from two glasses a night to one glass and introduced two alcohol-free days a week. That saved us about $40 a month.

We love going to the movies once a week so we invested in a book of discount tickets and joined two movie clubs which offered reduced rates at each session. I also swim every morning so I bought a book of season tickets which worked out cheaper than paying the full rate each visit and Steve joined a cheaper gym which saved us about $30 a month.

There are other ways to free up extra dollars. By planning ahead with meals and shopping, you will spend less at convenience stores. If you buy in bulk from supermarkets, you will enjoy further savings. Of course, eating out is a romantic time for many couples and cutting back on this luxury may seem too much of a sacrifice. But you could always buy some scented candles, try a new recipe and create a special atmosphere at home.

If you're renting and your lease is up for renewal, shop around for a better deal. If the rental market is stagnant, this puts you in a strong position and you may be able to negotiate a week's free rent or find a place offering the same or more facilities for less cost.

What to do with an extra $300 a month

- Pay more off your mortgage.
- Pay off credit card debts or personal loans.
- Set up an easy investment plan with a managed fund.
- Set up an education fund for your children.
- Salary sacrifice into superannuation.
- Organise a direct debit to go into a special holiday or Christmas account.

ULTIMATE BUDGETING TIPS

- *Treat sales with care.* Sales are notoriously risky for impulse buyers. If you are planning on shopping during this time, make a list of items you actually need before you go and stick to it. On the other hand, sales can also be a sensational time to make genuine savings. You can often buy next year's Christmas and birthday presents for family and friends at discounted prices which will save you money in the long run.
- *Rely on EFTPOS.* If you can take cash out when you make an EFTPOS purchase, it will count as only one transaction.
- *Consolidate accounts.* Do you have several bank accounts between you that can be consolidated to reduce monthly account-keeping fees? If so, visit your bank to discuss your options and find out about a savings account with a higher interest rate to help you save more.
- *Save regularly.* By making electronic transfers into a high-interest savings account, you will be surprised at how quickly your savings can accumulate.
- *Shop around.* Not just for food and clothing, but for interest rates, insurance, a new car, mobile telephone deals, and so on. Use the Internet to help you find the best deal. For example, the Website www.carquote.com can help you save thousands when buying a car. My husband tried it when shopping around to buy a car recently and managed to save more than $7000 on the best price quoted by a dealer without moving from his computer. Bond dealer FIIG Securities has a one-stop Website—www.termdeposit.com—where you can shop for interest rates on deposits from banks, credit unions and building societies. You can also make your deposit online using BPAY. Some of the rates are much better than you will find in your local bank branch, thanks to the Internet's lower costs. Before renewing your insurance, contact a few other companies to see what they are offering. You will be surprised at how much you can save with a minimum of effort.
- *Bank online.* Forget rushing to the bank and joining a queue to beat closing time. Bank online and you can pay your bills,

transfer funds between accounts and check your account balance 24 hours a day, seven days a week. Some banks even offer a 'pay anyone' facility which enables you to pay bills provided you have the company's necessary account details. Contact your institution about fees for this service.

- *Use your own bank's ATMs.* You may have to walk around the block to find it, but it will be worth the exercise as rival ATMs attract additional transaction fees.
- *Be a one-car family.* The cost of running an average family car up to five years old is $165.80 a week or $8621.60 a year, according to the NRMA. That includes depreciation, registration, insurance, road-service membership, interest on a car loan, fuel, the cost of replacing tyres and general maintenance. If you are a two-car family, it is a big outlay that can be put to better use, provided you can manage with just one set of wheels. So sit down and decide. If you need a car to ferry the children around, can your partner use public transport to travel to and from work? By selling that second car, you can use the funds to wipe out credit-card debts, reduce a mortgage, set up an investment strategy—or at least pay off the loan on your other car!
- *Pay bills electronically.* The electronic bill-paying option BPAY is growing rapidly in popularity, with more than 6000 participating organisations. It's a simple and efficient way to pay your bills. Australia Post's POSTbillpay gives consumers the option of paying bills in person, via the phone (13 18 16) or on the Internet at www.postbillpay.com.au.
- *Cut costs on lifestyle assets.* Many people may have over-committed themselves to property, with Australians in the past few years owing more on their mortgages than the country's foreign debt. If you are saving for a home, be realistic about how much you can afford. Too many people sacrifice their lifestyle for bricks and mortar, often to the detriment of their relationship. Perhaps you could manage in an apartment rather than a house or rent for a few more years. Apply the same thinking to cars too.
- *Access savings to cancel debt.* If you have spare funds sitting in a bank account attracting a woeful 0.02 per cent interest rate

while your credit card debt is attracting a whopping 15.75 per cent, withdraw the spare cash to cancel out your debt.

- *Make extra mortgage payments.* Say you have a $100 000 loan over a 25-year term at an interest rate of 7 per cent and monthly repayments of $707. If you continue making the same repayment for the full term, the total cost will be $212 034. Yet if you can stretch yourself to a further $50 a month, you will pay off your loan in 21 years. The total cost will be $191 681, a saving of $20 353. Alternatively, if you pay fortnightly, you will make the equivalent of thirteen monthly repayments a year. You will therefore pay your loan off in 20.5 years and save $23 000.
- *Get the best mobile phone deal.* There are almost 600 different plans on offer in Australia so you need to become well acquainted with how you use your mobile phone: the number of calls you make, the time of day you usually call, the average time you spend on calls and the type of calls you make—local, national or international. Examine your bills closely. Does your partner chat away, oblivious to the cost? Does the amount swing widely from month to month or are you consistent users? It may be worth your while for a trial period to take out a prepaid SIM card, which you can buy from a newsagent or service station, to find out if the network coverage is suitable. You can also visit the Website www.choice.com.au to help choose the best plan for you.

  It is essential to shop around using a cost checklist to find out whether you can afford a mobile phone deal and to ensure you make the right choice.

MOBILE PHONE CHECKLIST

The following checklist is great to have on hand when either of you are looking to buy a phone or if your children are in the market for a phone.

Read the contract carefully before signing, particularly the fine print. Some contracts are difficult to break, while others may require up to three months' payments to cancel. To help you find the best phone deal, simply fill in the following details.

How much is the phone?	$.....................
Cost of connection:	$.....................
Cost of disconnection:	$.....................
Monthly cost of fixed contract:	$.....................
How long is the contract for?	.... months
How much are call costs?	$.....................
Are the call costs at different rates for different times?	Yes/No
Is there an off-peak rate?	Yes/No
When is it?	....
How likely are we to use this?	....
How is the call charged: Per second? Per 30 seconds? Other?	....
Is there a minimum charge, even if the call is only for a few seconds?	Yes/No $
What are the call costs to different places?	
Within local area:	....
Interstate:	....
Overseas:	....
Is it cheaper to call mobiles from the same phone provider?	Yes/No
What do the extra features cost?	
SMS?	....
Do you pay to retrieve messages?	Yes/No
How much?	$
Do you pay when someone leaves a message?	Yes/No
Is there a minimum monthly payment?	Yes/No
Do you pay to use directory assistance?	Yes/No
Do you pay to use Message Bank?	Yes/No

Source: Ryde–Eastwood Financial Counselling Services

Once you have done your costing, it's time to look into the contract. A fixed-term contract means you will pay a fixed amount for the period of the agreement—usually eighteen months to two years. On the positive side, you may find that calls are cheaper with this type of contract because of the length of your deal.

With a fixed term, you nominate the minimum level you want to use each month—for example, $40 a month. If you use more than this amount you will be charged a higher rate, but if you use less than the $40 you will not get a refund.

Then there's pre-paid mobile phone accounts where you pay as you go, simply topping up your card as you require. This may be a better option for some people as there are no fixed monthly charges. But do your homework and don't forget to take the cost checklist with you.

If your family has two mobile phones, perhaps you should consider coping with just one. It could save you buckets of money and you probably won't miss it. Remember, there is always the public phone.

THE COST OF CREDIT

Putting all your spending on your credit card makes sense if you are one of those disciplined, savvy couples who always pay off the balance in full each month. They are also a convenient and sensible tool for travellers. But misusing a credit card is the easiest way to blow your budget—and many of us do, with statistics from independent Australian research house Cannex showing that in June 2002 Australians paid a total of $166 million in interest on outstanding credit card debt. And two-thirds of card users are unable to pay their bills on time. Here are some hints to help you take control:

- *Choose a card to match your financial situation.* Make sure that the credit card you use is the most suitable for your spending patterns. If you use your card for extended credit and don't pay off the balance in full each month, choose a card with a lower interest rate. It may not offer any interest-free period or loyalty programs, but the lower rate should save you more in the long run. If you use your credit card for the convenience of paying for everyday purchases such as petrol or groceries, try a credit or charge card with maximum interest-free days—

then make sure you pay it off in full each month. This way, you get the benefit of up to 55 interest-free days on purchases, as well as buyers' rewards, discounts and frequent flyer points. Or try a debit card that charges no interest but debits your savings account direct for your purchases. Check out the credit card selector at the Website www.bankchoice.com to find the cards that best suit your needs.

- *Avoid cash advances*. If you use your credit card to buy an item, you will get up to 55 days' interest-free credit. That's because you usually pay by the 20th of the following month. But it's a different story if you use it to withdraw money. From the day you make the withdrawal, you will pay compound interest of about 18 per cent. Ouch!
- *Be wary of interest-free periods*. In most cases, interest-free periods will not apply if you do not pay off the balance in full each month. If you have an outstanding balance from your last statement or just pay off the minimum amount each month, you will not get any interest-free benefits on your present and future purchases. With some cards, you will be penalised further if you don't pay off your balance in full by the due date by being charged interest from the actual date of purchase. In other words, you won't get the benefit of any interest-free period.
- *Focus on fees*. Fees are another area where you need to do your homework. Common fees include annual account fees, late payment fees, reward program fees, exceeding credit limit fees and payment dishonour fees.
- *One card or two*? Sure you can save money on annual fees by sharing one credit card, but if you have a secondary card for your partner, be aware that you are liable for any amounts owing. There are some institutions that do not cancel a secondary card until it has been returned to them. This decision will once again be determined by your financial personality types. If your partner keeps track of every cent you spend, you may need the independence that your own card brings. However, if you are both disciplined, pay off the balance in full each month and don't conduct post-mortems on each other's spending, one card may be enough.

YOUR CHILDREN'S EDUCATION

Some parents have been known to put down their child's name for private schooling in the precious few minutes after their baby is born. But if you're keen to join the drift to private education then you will need to start saving from that time too!

This trend is in defiance of the increasing costs of such an education. If patterns continue, parents of a millennium baby can expect to pay up to $40 000 for a child's secondary schooling in government high schools, double this amount in Catholic secondary colleges and up to five times this amount in private or independent schools, according to the Australian Scholarships Group, an independent provider of funds for parents to support children's education. This includes all costs—from fees and uniforms to travel and excursions. The estimates assume that fees and levies will continue to grow at 8 per cent annually and that other costs will rise by 5 per cent a year.

To cover the costs of an education in private or state schooling, it's best to start saving as soon as possible, even before your child's first birthday. From an initial investment of $1000, you will need to invest $1300 annually or about $110 a month up until age thirteen for a state secondary education; for a private education, it's $7170 a year or $600 a month until age thirteen. And that's just for one child!

If you already have commitments such as a mortgage, car payments and credit card debts, this may seem like an impossible task. But the longer you delay, the more it will cost.

For example, if you start saving for a state secondary education when your child turns seven, you will have to invest $4135 a year plus the initial $1000 or $435 a month for the next six years. If you are planning for private schooling, it will be $22 125 a year or $1845 a month.

In this model, by beginning when the child is in the nursery, you can save yourself up to $100 000. That's because by investing earlier you harness the power of compound interest.

So what are the best ways to get started? You could open a savings account in the name of the spouse with the lower income (or no income) to minimise your tax, then have a direct-debit arrangement where you contribute an amount each week or month. However, this option may not result in the best possible interest rate or outcome.

You can open a diversified managed fund for as little as $1000 that invests in a mix of assets such as shares, cash, property and fixed interest. You should also put this investment in the name of the lower-earning spouse.

If you prefer not to invest now, you can always pay for it out of your income when your child is ready to walk through the secondary school gates. Or you can borrow the money when you need it—but this is a costly solution. Both options may make it difficult to achieve longer term goals, such as using extra funds to top up your superannuation contributions.

Figure 5.1 Funding school fees: private secondary school

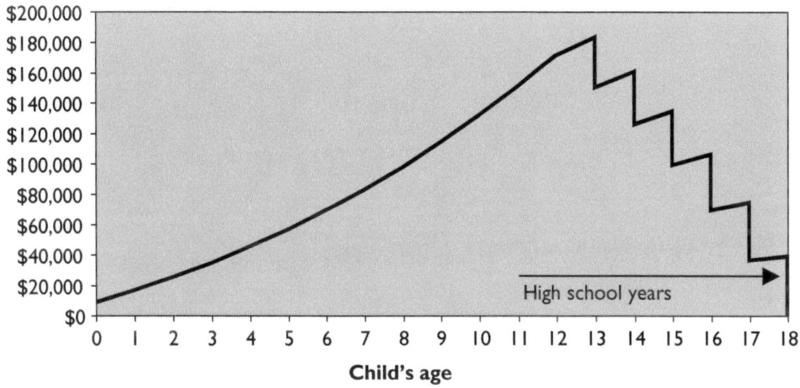

Source: BT Funds Management Limited. Assumptions: $1000 initial investment and regular investment of $7170 (indexed to inflation) at the end of each year. Post tax returns of 7% p.a. and 3% inflation. Regular investment begins when child is born and continues until age 13. Education costs of $33 500 p.a. (indexed) from age 13 to 18 inclusive. All investment earnings have been reinvested. No allowance has been made for tax or fees. The example is based on one set of assumptions and a small change in the assumptions can lead to a large change in results.

The message is: to ease the pressure of schooling costs, start to save sooner rather than later. As always, there's nothing like sound planning and budgeting to help you go the distance.

Visit the website at:

http://www.fido.asic.gov.au/fido/fido.nsf/byheadline/money+management?opendocument

You can either download or print out the spreadsheet under FIDO's Budget Planner or consult the Money Plan in Appendix I on page 216.

6

Be winners on one wage

Myth: No couple can win on one wage.
Fact: It's definitely tough, but it's achievable.

At some stage in your lives you may have reason to switch from the power of two to one wage. This may be the result of any one of a number of factors—from planned time out to have a baby to redundancy, illness, study or long-term unemployment.

Coping on one wage can test the best relationships. It may appear to be achievable at first, but mounting debts and additional expenses can leave you feeling out of control. If you find yourselves in this situation, you are not alone and there is always help available. This is also a time when you must make sure you are receiving all your entitlements, particularly if you are having a child.

According to Narelle Brown, coordinator of Ryde–Eastwood Financial Counselling Service, couples who seek financial assistance range from the very rich to the very poor. In fact, when things go wrong, those on higher incomes often find it more difficult to cope with managing their finances than those used to being on a tight budget.

Just how long you will have to survive on one wage will depend on your individual circumstances. But there is really no need to panic. You both can continue to be winners simply by minimising the financial impact on your lifestyle. Let's start with some commonsense strategies.

PRACTISE LIVING ON ONE INCOME

If you are thinking about having a baby or returning to study, making ends meet may seem like a daunting task. You may have even shelved the idea because it seems financially impossible.

One way of finding out whether you can survive without life's little extras is to have a trial run, which will enable you to iron out any unforeseen problems. Narelle Brown suggests that if you know in advance that you will be out of work, it's a good idea to visit a counsellor to get some advice to help with the preparations:

> There is a small percentage of couples who know their income is going to change. Perhaps they are about to have a baby and they know they will have to cope on the one wage. Those couples often come in and we do a money plan on what their income is going to be.
>
> It is just surprising what a basic money plan offers them because they don't think of the little things that they spend their money on. Putting it down on paper is probably the first time they have actually seen it. For example, they may have a gym membership that they aren't using. They may go to the hairdresser every few weeks. They may be smokers, which can be really expensive at around $8 a packet.

Doing a money plan (see Appendix 1, page 216) takes about two hours. It is not an answer to poverty, but it will provide valuable information about costs and choices.

The trick is to make sure you first set aside money to cover essential expenses, such as rent, electricity and insurance. Then detail other expenses for food, pocket money, entertainment and so on. Don't be surprised if you get to the end and find yourself in the red. Go back to the non-essentials and determine what you can live without.

You may find that you will really struggle on one wage and that you need to delay your decision to take time out for another year or so. But it is better to have found out during a practice run than by plunging into a dark, dollar-starved reality unaware of what you will be up against.

This happened to Kristy and Luke. They had no income

worries when they were both working. Without thinking too much about the financial consequences, they began trying for their first baby. With all their possessions—house, furniture, two cars—they were sure they could manage and not want for anything.

It might mean they would have to juggle one wage and do without overseas holidays for a while. But that's all—or so they thought. Their house had risen in value to $450 000 and their mortgage was $250 000 with repayments of $1800 a month. Their credit cards were up to $12 000, requiring a minimum repayment of $360 a month.

When the baby arrived, the supermarket bill was substantial—all those nappies and cleaning products cost much more than they had anticipated—so the credit card bill grew close to $14 000 and repayments climbed to $420.

One wage of $3000 a month, less the mortgage payment of $1800, less the credit card payment of $420, left only $195 a week for food, petrol, water, electricity, insurance, etc. All of a sudden, life became really difficult.

Kristy thought of putting the baby into child care and getting a part-time job. But it didn't seem worth it and, anyway, it was not what they wanted. The government's baby bonus came just in time to cover the car insurance, while the maternity allowance was also devoted to outstanding bills.

But just when you think things can only get better, they can suddenly get much worse. Luke's company was forced to close and he was left without a job. Holiday pay kept the family going for about six weeks, then he had to apply for a special unemployment allowance.

Luke felt sure he would easily get a new job, but after applying for many positions he was disheartened. The bills kept coming, the baby was irritable with teething, Kristy was distressed and he felt like a failure.

Soon they were skipping the mortgage payments to pay for the credit cards and other bills to get them through. Then they would miss the credit card payments to pay the mortgage. Finally, they were three months in arrears on their loan and the bank threatened legal action.

That's when a friend suggested they seek help from a free financial counsellor, who provided a number of options to sort out their situation in the short term. In the meantime, Luke was given breathing room to find work. First, the mortgage was researched but, since they were already on a good rate, refinancing was not an option. An application was made for mortgage assistance which, in New South Wales, is a state-funded program to assist people to stay in their homes after suffering unforeseen circumstances. It is paid by way of an interest-free loan of up to $10 000 directly onto the mortgage. The main condition was that they had to pay 27 per cent of their income to the loan as well as meet other criteria.

The financial counsellor then contacted their credit card providers for a moratorium on repayments for a period of three months with token payments of $50 a month. Luke and Kristy were shown how to prepare a budget and manage their tight income. This gave them the space they needed to get things back in order.

Luke soon found a good job and gradually their life returned to normal. The mortgage assistance loan was repaid, the credit cards were converted to a personal loan with a much lower interest rate and were repaid each month. One card with a small limit was maintained and drawings were kept to a minimum to ensure that they could be debt-free (apart from their home loan) in three years. Their aim was never to have to experience this situation again.

PAYING THE MORTGAGE

One of the biggest outlays couples face is their mortgage repayment. The thought of moving to one wage and still meeting that dreaded monthly commitment can be frightening for some.

While you have the benefit of two wages, plan to pay off more than you need so that your time on one wage is less stressful.

When one of my friends recently took maternity leave, she and her husband had been paying in excess of their required mortgage repayments for a number of years simply by paying fortnightly. Not only did this help cushion them from rising interest rates, it allowed them to reduce their repayments to a bare minimum throughout her time off, which was comforting when they were only bringing in one wage.

If you are paying your mortgage fortnightly and are unsure of how much extra you have paid off, speak to your financial

How to cut costs

- Make fortnightly payments on your mortgage.
- Pay for your electricity fortnightly and your insurance premiums monthly. This will smooth out larger payments and remove nasty surprises.
- Pay as many bills as you can via the telephone or Internet—this will save you money on stamps, envelopes and cheques.
- Check that you have the most cost-effective mobile telephone plan to suit your usage, limit calls or get rid of the mobile altogether.
- If you are paying for private health insurance, shop around to make sure you have the best deal to meet your needs. Are you using any extra cover or can you switch to a cheaper plan?
- If you have cable television, consider cancelling your subscription. You can always renew it when your dual-income capacity is restored.
- If you have an expensive car, examine the options. Could you buy a second-hand car? Or a cheaper new car? Could you manage as a one-car family by relying on public transport and the odd taxi?
- Shop around for home, car and contents insurance when your policies come up for renewal.
- School fees can be a killer so divide the annual cost into a monthly amount and invest it each month in an interest-bearing account.
- Buy school equipment in bulk through supermarket chains or office-supply stores. Blank exercise books can be bought in a book pack from high-school canteens, most of which will be run by the P&C.
- Do your grocery shopping online and in bulk. This may incur a small delivery fee but you will avoid unnecessary items you are tempted to buy at the supermarket because they are on special or catch your eye. Try to buy fruit and vegetables that are in season. The others will only hit your hip pocket.
- Join your local library to access books, music and videos. There are even toy libraries.

institution. Perhaps you can cease payments for a few months then move back to the minimum amount until you return to two wages.

HOW TO ASK YOUR PARTNER FOR MONEY

If one partner is earning an income, the non-earning spouse will more than likely feel financially dependent upon the other. No one wants to feel as though they need to ask their partner for a handout every time they want to buy something. This can be a difficult issue, particularly if both have been earning a wage then all of a sudden one isn't. You may have thought nothing of buying yourself a new outfit, whereas now you may feel the need to sneak it into your wardrobe, cutting off the price tag on the way. This is a time when the sole income earner needs to be extra sensitive towards their partner's new situation.

Don't let this issue slide, hoping that things will work themselves out. Sit down together and sort out a solution to suit both of you.

Stuart and Liz found themselves in this situation when she left work after twelve years in the job she loved to do further study. First, they went back to their budget to determine how much she needed for general household costs and her own personal expenses. They then agreed on a monthly figure and the manner in which she would be paid. There were several options. The money could be debited directly to her own bank account, saving her the embarrassment of having to ask for it or remind her sometimes forgetful partner to transfer the funds. Or it could simply be deposited in their joint account, and she could withdraw it at the agreed time.

Liz opted to have the money directly debited into her account just as she did with her own salary when she was working. That way she felt more in control of her affairs.

HONEY, CAN WE AFFORD THE KIDS?

The birth of a first child is occurring later and later as couples continue to postpone this key decision in their lives. Social

Table 6.1 Estimated average costs of a single child, by age of child and family income

Level of income	Average income $pw	Age of child 0 to 4 $pw	5 to 9 $pw	10 to 14 $pw	15 to 17 $pw	18 to 24 $pw
Low income	567	55	98	130	213	215
Middle income	1,195	95	156	199	305	309
High income	2,426	167	255	315	458	466

Source: NATSEM Income & Wealth Report, March 2002

researcher Hugh Mackay labels this post-30 group 'the postponement generation'. Not only are they putting off having children, but they are taking longer to walk down the aisle, buy a home and get serious about money. It's all about choices. They may choose to have a child or they may not, as the declining birth rate of 1.7 babies per female reveals.

There is also the big issue of cost, with research finding the cost for the average Australian couple of raising two children from birth to 20 is almost $450 000 in total, or $310 per week, according to the National Centre for Social & Economic Modelling 2002 Income and Wealth Report. From birth to age four, a low-income family forks out $55 a week, a middle-income family about $95 and a high-income family $167 for a single child.

These costs may sound outrageous but once you are forewarned you can plan together to minimise the impact on your budget. You can make an informed decision about private health insurance, set up a savings plan, source secondhand furniture where possible (www.tradingpost.com.au or www.sold.com.au), and start slowly accumulating what you will need from the moment you confirm your pregnancy. When I had my son, Wilton, I had no idea how much he would cost to bring into the world. Here is a brief rundown of the *bare* basics:

Raising Wilton

Six-week ante-natal class:	$110
Visits and delivery by obstetrician in private hospital:	$3000 to $5000
or	
Three-day public hospital stay with midwife delivery:	free
Disposable nappies:	$24 per week
Formula:	2 @ $18 each per week
Clothing:	$400 (jumpsuits, singlets, bibs, tops etc.)
Nursery fit-out:	$700 (change table, cot, baby monitor, bedding)
Car seat:	$350
Pram:	$300
Baby bath:	$50

And, of course, there are the ongoing costs of raising a child. If you have the luxury of planning your children, take advantage of the situation and reduce as many debts as you can. Being prepared gives you a head start. I might add that, putting aside the financial implications, he has been worth every cent! The worksheet from BabyCo on page 74 is a helpful checklist if you are planning a baby, but remember that not all the items on the checklist are 'must-have's'.

YOUR CHILD CARE OPTIONS

The cost of child care can bite deeply into the pay packet and single-income families will feel the pinch even more.

While family, grandparents and friends may be the cheapest child-minding option, they are not always available, leaving parents to weigh the costs of long day care, occasional care, in-home care, outside school hours' care, family day care, preschools or even a nanny.

In selecting the best option, parents obviously need to consider whether they prefer their children to be in a home-like environment among a small group of children or in a larger centre with qualified staff. The location of child care will also be a key factor, especially if you have employer-based care or the centre is on your way to and from work.

Then there's the cost. This will vary depending on whether your service is run privately, by a local council or by a community-based organisation. To ease the burden, Australian families are eligible for the Child Care Benefit and Child Care Rebate, which is an income-based assessment—so the more you earn, the more you will pay for child care. If you have a large family, a nanny may prove more cost effective while a child care centre may suit smaller families. Family day care—where there is just one adult looking after a small number of children in the carer's home—may be the cheapest option for working parents. But this service may not suit everyone, especially those who prefer greater social interaction for their children.

In many cases, the cost of child care or a nanny can be as much as the second wage earner is bringing home. However, some parents find that returning to work gives them the mental stimulation they need and that the time they spend with their kids, although limited, is of better quality.

But juggling work, family and the home is not an easy task—as any parent who has done it will tell you. You need to do the sums and decide what is right for both of you.

- For information on quality child care, visit the National Childcare Accreditation Council's Website www.ncac.gov.au or call (02) 8260 1900 or 1300 136 554 (for callers outside Sydney).
- To help you select the right type of child care for you and your child, call the Child Care Access Hotline on 1800 670 305.
- To find out about the Child Care Benefit and Child Care Rebate, contact your local Centrelink office on 131021; for family tax benefits, visit the Website www.familyassist.gov.au or phone 136150 to find out where your nearest Family Assistance Office is located.
- To find out the cost of hiring a nanny, visit www.dial-an-angel.com or www.nanniesandhelpers.com.au

Baby Budget Worksheet

Car Safety

Several types of child restraints are available. A suitable restraint will depend on your child's age, size and weight.

- Capsule (0 to approx six months) $.......
- Convertible car seat (0 to approx four years) $.......
- Car seats (six months to approx four years) $.......
- Booster seats $.......

Car Safety Accessories

- ☐ Extra bolt for second car
- ☐ 'Baby On Board' stickers
- ☐ Capsule sun hood
- ☐ Window sun shades
- ☐ Extension straps for hatch-backs, station wagons and four-wheel drives

Going Out

For a new baby you will need comfortable transport, where they can rest or safely play.

- Fully reclinable pram/stroller (from birth) $.......
- Stroller from six months $....
- Portable cot/playpen $.......
- ☐ Mosquito net
- ☐ Rain cover
- ☐ Wool liner
- ☐ Bottle/carrier warmer
- ☐ Cuddle bag
- ☐ Pram blanket
- ☐ Pram toys
- ☐ Back pack
- ☐ Nappy bag
- ☐ Sun shade cloth
- ☐ Portable change mat

Nursery Furniture

- Cot $.......
- Chest of drawers $.......
- Cot halo stand and ring $.....
- Cradle/bassinette, stand, crook $.......
- Glider rocking chair (great for feeding) $.......
- Ottoman for resting those tired feet $.......

Nursery Manchester

- Cot pillows $.......
- Mattress (inner spring or block foam) $.......
- 2 x mattress protectors $....
- 3 x sheet sets $.......
- 2 x winter blankets $.......
- 2 x summer blankets$.......
- 3 x piece quilt set $.......
- ☐ Cot halo net
- ☐ Tetra snuggle bed
- ☐ Nappy stacker
- ☐ Mobiles for visual stimulation

Cradle/Bassinette

- Tetra or foam mattress $.....
- 3 x sheet sets $.......
- 2 x blankets $.......
- Quilt and liner set $.......

Bath & Change Time

- Change table station $.....
- Change table $.....
- Bath and stand $.....
- ☐ Bathing aids
- ☐ Bath thermometer
- ☐ Bath towels x 4
- ☐ Change pad/mat

Baby Budget Worksheet

- ☐ Wash mittens x 2
- ☐ Nappy buckets
- ☐ Face washers x 6
- ☐ Cloth nappies (two dozen)
- ☐ Hooded towels x 2
- ☐ Nappy pins
- ☐ Bath seat/safety ring

Hungry Baby Needs

- ■ High chair (from approx six months) $.......
- ■ High chair insert $.......
- ■ Portable high chair $.......

Other Essentials

- ☐ Hand/battery breast pump
- ☐ Microwave or electric sterilisers
- ☐ Feeding bottles
- ☐ Bibs
- ☐ Training mugs
- ☐ Soft spoons
- ☐ Suction toys for high chair trays
- ☐ Lamp
- ☐ Night lights
- ☐ Rattles and soft toys
- ☐ Potty
- ☐ Scissors/baby clippers
- ☐ Carry pouch
- ☐ Sheep skin bunny rug

$......

Exercisers

- ☐ Balla balla
- ☐ Jolly jumper
- ☐ Baby swing
- ☐ Rocker carry chair
- ☐ Baby walker
- ☐ Bouncer
- ☐ Activity gym

$.......

Home Safety

- ■ Child-proof power outlet plugs $.......
- ■ Cupboard door locks $.......
- ■ Door barrier $.......
- ■ VCR lock $.......
- ■ Stairway gate $.......
- ■ Refrigerator latch $.......
- ■ Stove guard $.......
- ■ Corner cushions $.......
- ■ Monitor: complete convenient monitoring of your baby's sounds $.......

YOUR NOTES

___

___

___

INCOME PROTECTION INSURANCE

Expect the unexpected in life and you will never be surprised. You can never tell if you will suddenly find yourselves in a situation that prevents you from earning an income due to sickness or an accident. You can usually obtain income protection insurance that will cover up to 75 per cent of your income if you fall ill within the guidelines of the policy. Presumably, you won't need 100 per cent of your salary because you are less likely to be dining out, buying a new working wardrobe or going to shows. It is also fully tax deductible. For more details, see Chapter 13.

7

Dealing with baggage

Myth: My partner doesn't seem to have any baggage.
Fact: Everyone comes with some sort of baggage, whether it's from past relationships, family or life experiences.

Wherever you go in life, have you noticed how you are always carrying something? When you go to work, it's a bag or briefcase. When you travel, it's a suitcase. When you have children, it's the baby. Or when you shop, it's a wallet.

A relationship is no different. Here, you will also carry plenty of baggage—only it will be mostly of the emotional and financial kind, which can be just as heavy and as portable as the bags you bring home from the supermarket.

Inside this personal baggage come issues that can't be ignored. Such as how do you cope if your partner has children from a prior relationship? How do you juggle maintenance and a mortgage? How do you decide whose place to live in? And how do you determine who pays for what?

As you sort through this baggage, try to keep in mind that you, as a couple, have the power of two. You have double the earning capacity so you should have double the savings and investment potential. Even if a partner brings serious financial commitments to your relationship, it is possible to work around them. Open communication, understanding and planning are the keys. A sensible budget (see Chapter 5) is a good place to start and will help you through the toughest of times, ensuring you have enough in the kitty to enjoy life now and in the future.

But be aware that how you deal with emotional baggage can make or break your relationship. Obviously, the more secure you feel with a partner, the better equipped you will be to deal with matters lugged from the past into the present.

WHO PAYS FOR WHAT?

This may depend on your early dating patterns, the individual earning capacity of each of you and your strengths and weaknesses with money. I know a couple who split everything—from utilities to dining out—down the middle. This pattern was established from their first date and they have maintained it for fourteen years.

Take a moment to think back to that first date. Did your partner automatically pay for you or did you go Dutch? Often, early dating behaviour will have a profound effect on the way you both deal with finances. Perhaps your partner is tired of paying for everything, as this is what happened in a previous relationship, whereas you may have split everything but now want someone to look after you.

Of course, how you meet your day-to-day expenses will depend on your personal circumstances and what works best for you. If you are better at paying bills on time, take responsibility for that role and decide who will pay for what. Maybe you will take turns at paying for everything. You may prefer to split any bills or one person may pay for the lot. The key is not to squabble over this issue, but to sit down and discuss what you consider to be fair and sensible.

Regardless of your experiences and expectations, be prepared to compromise. On the other hand, if your new partner has plenty of money in the bank but refuses to put hand in pocket, you may need to provide a dose of reality. If you are entering into a relationship, you have to have a level of trust and a willingness to give, says psychologist Susan Nicholson:

> If one person is stingy and concerned about holding on to a little piece of the pie, that is a warning sign. If the other feels they are being controlled in that way, they should speak up and address it and not just run with it.

If you look at what couples argue about, money is usually the biggest source of tension and more complicated the second time around. If you are arguing a lot about money, you may need to look at what is going on at an emotional level.

PRE-EXISTING ASSETS

When you enter a new relationship, you usually bring with you different assets such as bank account savings, property, shares and even debt. You also need to deal with a new partner's expectations of what is 'yours' and what is 'ours'. Some people believe that once a relationship is established, everything that is yours is also theirs. Without getting into a huge argument, how do you deal with this issue in a mature way?

You need to be honest about your views on this. Without open, frank discussion, many wrong assumptions could be made by a new partner. If you want your assets to remain separate from those of your partner, you must say so. If this is important to you, your new partner will need to understand that the baggage from your past relationship may be the driving factor and will need to respect this.

PRE-NUPTIAL AGREEMENTS

Often, a suggestion from a new partner to enter a pre-nuptial agreement can help ease the pain of a past experience. If there is little emphasis placed on pre-existing assets by the new partner, the sheer act of signing an agreement allows the relationship to start on solid ground.

Pre-nuptial agreements are still a relatively new concept. In Australia, amendments to the *Family Law Act* passed on 27 December 2000 make them legally binding. No longer a Clayton's agreement, they are attracting more interest, particularly for couples marrying for a second time or for people bringing significant personal or family assets to a marriage—including those involved in family businesses who wish to protect their holdings.

In the first relationship, people tend to be blindly in love with few assets so the playing field is even. In the next marriage, people are still in love but a bit more worldly. There may be children from a first marriage to whom they are keen to bequeath assets rather than have them end up in the hands of their new partner's family.

If you are asked to sign a pre-nuptial, try to be understanding, not insulted. Deal with the issue in a calm manner. Make sure your needs are covered, but realise that the assets are more than likely to have been accumulated in a different time and place.

Changes to superannuation laws have resulted in retirement savings becoming a key part of pre-nuptial agreements, says Robert Benjamin, an accredited family law specialist with Watts McCray family lawyers:

> So far they are appealing more to people entering a second marriage who have been through the process and are quite happy to live happily ever after provided their assets are safeguarded.
>
> Contrary to what many people may think, this is not a male-dominated area and just as many women are interested in pre-nuptials as men. Often, women, especially from the baby-boomer generation, very much value security and they do not want to put that at risk by marrying someone without such an agreement, particularly when the statistics state that more than one in three marriages end in divorce.

To be binding, pre-nuptial agreements must be in writing, with full financial disclosure, signed by both parties and accompanied by a confirmation from solicitors that both parties understand the agreement and have received independent legal advice. It is recommended that such agreements be drawn up by solicitors. 'They are not hard to get into and they do not need court approval,' Benjamin says. 'But there are some fairly good exit provisions.'

Examples where such agreements can be set aside by a court include cases where the circumstances surrounding the care of a child have changed. A pre-nuptial agreement will also be tested if there has been fraud or non-disclosure of assets when setting it up or if 'unconscionable conduct' is involved—such as forcing it to be signed on the wedding day. To be effective, it must be fair and stand the test of time. But, as Benjamin warns, what may be fair for the first five years of a relationship may not be fair for the next 30 years:

> Pre-nuptials allow people to make up their own minds about their destiny as long as they are thoughtful and careful about it. A pre-nuptial could allow for changes over time by, for example, dividing property differently depending on how long the marriage has lasted. With the dynamics of the ageing generation, the male is often the big income earner and that can lend itself to poverty for the wife if the marriage breaks down. Men have tended to recover fairly quickly, financially speaking, but there are some sad examples of men who never recover from family law.

If you want a pre-nuptial agreement, be aware that it may be an awkward, sensitive subject to raise with your partner. But don't be put off. It may be even more awkward in the long term if you don't proceed. Neither party should let something as practical as a pre-nuptial come between them.

Even if no such agreement is involved, couples still need to sit down and discuss, calmly and frankly their financial situation and how they intend to deal with pre-existing. For example, if you have a substantial amount in savings, you may not wish to combine this with your new partner's assets, especially if you have suffered a bad experience from a previous relationship. You may wish to have a joint account for your mortgage and a separate account for your own savings.

Or you may be happy to combine everything. This may also mean you can use your joint holdings to become more financially successful.

SEPARATE VERSUS JOINT ACCOUNTS

Once you have agreed on how to deal with pre-existing assets, you need to discuss whether or not to have separate bank accounts. Once again, past baggage will undoubtedly creep into the discussion so take off your emotional hat and don your business one. People deal with this in different ways, according to Anne Hollonds, chief executive of Relationships Australia in New South Wales and Victoria.

Increasingly, people are keeping things separate. If you do end that new relationship then it's much clearer who brought what into the marriage and, if you have been together 20 years, sifting through the paperwork can be a nightmare.

People tend to be more comfortable with separate accounts, particularly if there is a big differential in what one partner's bringing in versus the other. It's more sensible, but it can create some sense of bad feeling and that must be dealt with. If one partner wants to keep it separate and it's causing friction then that is something you will need to discuss in terms of what does this mean for your relationship.

Sometimes your past baggage may mean you give out mixed messages to your partner. By suggesting separate bank accounts, your partner may feel you are not fully committed to the relationship, which can cause insecurity and unnecessary pain.

Says Hollonds:

> It could be something that is entirely misunderstood; it could be that he or she is misreading signals. In fact, it could be that the other partner is unknowingly giving out mixed messages with what they are doing. Their new partner continues to feel insecure so it could be that they need to change something about what they are doing in order to demonstrate better to their partner that they are committed to them, that they love them, that they are special to them.
>
> So often when you examine why couples are having counselling, it comes down to this very thing. Somehow we always get that bit wrong. All of us to a greater or lesser extent are insecure and we are looking for reassurance, we are looking for a sense of safety in the relationship, and some of us can be sensitive to signals that might mean that really he or she is not committed. You have got to sort this out earlier on in the relationship. It comes down to what communication is going to work in that relationship and not making assumptions about why people act the way they do.

Some couples find that a joint account for joint expenses and separate accounts for their personal spending works best. If you want extra insurance in case the relationship sours, insist on being joint signatories for a joint account. By having joint and separate accounts, pre-existing assets can be accounted for neatly and both parties can still contribute financially to the new relationship.

However, what might be appropriate now may change down the track with, for example, the birth of a child. It may then be necessary to review your arrangements.

WHOSE HOUSE TO LIVE IN

Houses are not just bricks and mortar. They carry memories and a sense of possession. No matter how determined they are to create the space as their own, the person moving in may feel they have less of a sense of ownership. They may even feel like a guest in their partner's home, but are reluctant to say so.

If it is financially feasible, consider selling up and buying or renting something else together. If that's not an option, try to rearrange the place to make it a different space for the two of you. The problem may not be the house, but the furnishings and finishings. If that is the case, your solution is a lot simpler—and cheaper—than having to bid at an auction and meet costly expenses such as stamp duty.

Let's face it—your home is like a sanctuary from outside pressures and if you feel uncomfortable or resentful every time you walk through the front door then you should do something about it.

CHILDREN COME FIRST

If you have entered into a partnership where there are children from previous relationships, it is important to remember that, whatever happens, the children must always come first. Try not to analyse why or try to change it. It is a fact and should be understood from the first day of your life together.

There is no point telling your new partner that, when the

chips are down, he or she will have to choose between you and the kids. Leave ultimatums out of it, otherwise you may find yourself facing life alone. Unlike relationships, which can come and go, there is a special connection between parent and child that can never—and should never—be broken.

Susan Nicholson says it is vital for couples to go into a relationship with their eyes wide open, and not resent a partner fulfilling their obligations—both parental and financial—to their offspring:

> You must recognise that your partner is required legally and morally to support their children and you should not make an argument of it. Try to put yourself into their ex's shoes and come to terms with the fact that you have gone into a relationship aware of their commitments and that it can never be ignored.
>
> If their dad wants to pay school fees or shout them a bike or dress for their formal, butt out. Children need to come first and new partners, if they don't have children, won't understand the level of financial and emotional nurturing that is required. As long as he is not buying their love and just wants to do the best by his children then you should be doing all you can to support that.

MAINTENANCE MATTERS

If your partner is paying maintenance for children, it is easy to resent this outlay. If it's a lot, it may even feel like you're forking out the equivalent of a second mortgage.

Again, always remember that you as a couple have the power of two. So use this power. Sit down and talk about the issue, draw up a flexible budget, be aware of how the commitment will affect your finances and, if necessary, see a financial planner.

Anne Hollonds speaks from experience when she describes this as a tricky area as there is often a great deal of resentment. For many people, paying maintenance is an obstacle they face and it colours all the interactions that follow and it can actually get in the way of their relationships with their children. It used to be harder in the days when you created your new family—there was a desire to leave everything else outside that and to pretend it didn't exist so that this new family was the only family that existed and that everything else was intruding upon it. Thankfully, with so many people now moving in and out of relationships, at least it is something that can be discussed: this is a fact of our lives and how will we accommodate it. But that's not to say it doesn't cause arguments.

So how does a parent deal with this issue with a new partner? The sooner the better, Hollonds says. There may be a real fear of turning off your prospective partner but the good news is that people these days tend to have a more sophisticated attitude to the whole issue. So if you are going out with someone with kids, male or female, then there are issues relating to that family they are bringing with them and it would be unwise of someone to try to pretend that it wasn't going to affect the relationship in a whole lot of ways.

If there are kids involved, she says you have to be flexible and resilient within yourself and not take things personally.

It actually requires quite a level of emotional maturity for people to manage that sort of transition from no kids to kids. Couples need to have excellent communication skills to cope with issues such as managing money as well as managing multiple complex relationships with ex-partners and children.

Sometimes the partner may feel the need to be secretive about the amount of money being paid to an ex with custody of the children. They may not want their new partner to know what they are paying so as not to upset them or cause an argument. They may be paying above the odds because they feel guilty or because they just want the best for their offspring. Try to be supportive and understand their predicament. Put yourself in the ex's shoes and in your partner's shoes. If that were your child, wouldn't you want the best too? How would you feel if you had to justify every cent you spent?

If there is secrecy about maintenance—and money in general—be aware that this will most certainly create feelings of mistrust, if not now then further down the track. So try to be open about what and how much is being paid. If necessary, suggest a separate bank account for the payments to keep the peace.

DEMANDS FOR MORE

Sometimes, extra demands are placed on new couples for additional funds for children outside any court agreement. This can happen for many reasons. It may be that one partner wants to punish the other for leaving or is unable to let go emotionally. It may also be that the arrangements are unfair and the request is entirely legitimate. Whatever the reason, it can be easy to become bitter and twisted about a partner having to pay more when you are both madly saving for a home or even a holiday. Hollonds warns:

> If you are locked into a certain type of interaction that is repeated again and again, this may be a sign that you haven't been able to get into the ex's shoes sufficiently. You haven't understood how they see the world sufficiently to alter your way of dealing with them. Sometimes you can't get it right.

A counsellor can help couples talk through some of the reasons why the ex may be making more financial demands. This will help to increase their level of understanding and allow them to develop strategies to deal with the issue. And, by working together, they can only strengthen their own relationship. But Hollonds points out that a perfect solution is not always possible:

> Of course, at the other extreme, there are people who refuse to respond to anything. So you might have tried all these techniques, have got some professional advice, tried to approach them in a whole lot of different ways and they are still being difficult. It's really because they have been unable to come to terms with the change in circumstances and are unable to get on with their own life. They are stuck. And at the end of the day, if it is destructive to your new situation and to you, you need to put up some boundaries. Not everyone can come around to acting in a civil fashion.

Once again, in circumstances like these, it may even be necessary to invite a professional third party to help reinforce what the issues are and what the solutions could be. Whatever the reason, try to apply constructive communication skills rather than lashing out and having an argument or heading straight to the courts.

The same applies if guilt is involved. Your partner may happily hand over extra funds without giving it a second thought, and such behaviour may well stem from guilt. According to Hollonds, there are good reasons for people feeling guilty. They may well have been unfaithful in the marriage and be trying to compensate for that. That can be tricky financially. If you can afford it and it's not having an adverse impact on your new relationship, it may not be an issue. But if in fact it is, it becomes an issue for that new couple to address. In that situation, you need professional advice.

THE COSTS KEEP COMING

Imagine your child is nearing the age of eighteen, the usual time—depending on any legal agreement, of course—when your financial commitments are drawing to an end. In your mind, you may have quietly spent the money you have been setting aside for maintenance many times over.

You may think you will be off the hook financially, but are you? The reality is that the costs never really stop with a child. In fact, some of the larger costs emerge after the age of eighteen, especially if they go to university. And, of course, sometimes people's circumstances change. You and your partner might think that this is what you are buying into, this is the set of circumstances, then a few years later some things change. Or perhaps the level of support you are getting might dry up.

Again, if you are the one watching your partner forking out money for a 25-year-old daughter, you may have to put yourself in their shoes and try to understand. Perhaps your partner does need to step back and allow the adult offspring to be independent. Or perhaps the solution is to set aside a small amount of money each year to allow for these types of outlays. This comes back to the importance of open communication and keeping a budget so that you will know how much you are saving and how much you are spending.

Take the example of a woman and her partner who are keen to travel for two years when his daughter turns eighteen. Knowing how much he loves his only child, she has suggested putting aside a certain amount each year to fund an airfare in their travel budget so that the daughter can meet up with them along the way. He has scoffed at the idea, but deep down she knows this will be the wisest thing to do. Otherwise, he will miss her like mad and they may even have to cut short their trip or change their itinerary. It may mean staying in two-star rather than three-star hotels, but it will be a small sacrifice to pay to keep all parties smiling.

If you are juggling maintenance and other money issues, put on your business cap and, if necessary, seek financial advice on how best to manage the situation. Set and review goals and provide feedback so that you can make the most of your life together.

8

Get rich with bricks

Myth: There is no way we will ever be able to afford a home.
Fact: As a couple, you have the power of two. That means twice the saving—and buying—capacity.

There comes a stage in most couple's lives when they are keen to take the plunge into the property market. Perhaps it is the comfort of knowing that you are actually paying something off instead of spending your hard-earned cash on rent—and helping to pay off someone else's mortgage. Or you may regard it as a method of enforced saving. Perhaps it is the joy of not having to be at the whim of a faceless landlord who won't extend your six-month lease because it's a prime time to sell. It could be the need for something to call your own if you have a young family or you are planning one. Or maybe it is because both sets of parents keep nagging you about settling down and buying something.

Whatever the reasons, property is a long-term, emotional and financial investment for you as a couple. As well as your home being free of capital gains tax, it is a good feeling to know that as long as you play your cards right, you will have a roof over your head throughout your lives.

Buying a home is likely to be the biggest investment you will ever make. A home will also probably take you the longest to own of all your possessions.

That's all the more reason to make sure you get it right the first time. By spending plenty of time examining your options, ensuring you have a sizeable deposit and the most suitable loan, then selecting the suburb and style of home that will give you the most pleasure, you can help set yourselves up for life. Your financial personalities will also determine the type of property you buy and the amount you spend. Thrillseeker may want the inner-city waterfront apartment while steady would rather settle for the three-bedroom brick home in the surburbs.

However, like investing in the sharemarket, property does have its risks. If you find the home of your dreams and omit to check with the local council on zoning or any development plans, for instance, you may find that a large block of flats has been approved next door, blocking out any sunlight and your view. Or if you decide not to get that building inspection done on the home you've set your heart on, you may find that small crack in the corner of the lounge room turns into a gaping financial hole.

But if you do your homework, don't over-stretch yourselves on price and buy in an area that has good amenities and proximity to public transport and schools, your investment should bring you plenty of satisfaction.

Of course, your own home shouldn't make up your entire investment portfolio, particularly if you are looking for an income stream. Diversification is one of the most important aspects of becoming a financially successful couple so, if you can afford it, remember to take out that savings plan, diversifying in Australian and overseas shares, keep some money in fixed interest (cash and term deposits) for emergencies and top up your superannuation to ensure you have a balanced portfolio of assets.

CAN YOU AFFORD IT?

Saving up the deposit for a home loan is often the hardest part but, as a couple, you can get there faster thanks to the power of two. At the time of writing, if you are both first home buyers, you can boost your purchasing power with a one-off payment of $7000 from the federal government. For further details, check out the Website www.firsthome.gov.au.

Be aware, though, that having the required deposit of 10 per cent of the value of the property (if buying at auction) will not be enough. Other hidden costs, including stamp duty, conveyancing, building and pest inspections, and building and contents insurance, all must be considered.

Allow extra if you have to pay mortgage insurance, which is usually incurred when you borrow more than 80 per cent. This one-off payment protects the bank—not you—in case you default on your repayments. Some banks will add this fee to a loan so the client doesn't have to pay it upfront.

As a general rule, you need to allow at least a further 5 per cent of the value of the property on top of your deposit to cover the above-mentioned costs.

Remember, the more vigorous you are at saving for a deposit, the closer you will be to becoming home owners. Having two wages working for you should get you there faster.

YOUR HOME LOAN CHOICES

With more than 3000 types of home loans available, it is no wonder choosing the right home loan is a daunting task. But you can reduce the time and energy you spend on the task by first deciding what you are looking for. Do you want a 'no-frills' loan that just looks at the interest rate? Or are you happy to pay a slightly higher interest rate for extra features and flexibility, such as having your salaries paid into your home loan account?

You may find that loans with loads of features will cost you more in the long run, so be aware of what you are paying for. For example, loans such as a 'honeymoon special' will certainly give you a couple of years at a low interest rate but you may find the rate you end up with when the honeymoon is over is not all that competitive.

A good way of finding out just how much you will be paying for a home loan is to make use of what is known as the annualised average percentage rate (AAPR). Along with the advertised interest-rate, the AAPR takes into account all upfront and continuing fees. It means investors can benefit from clarity and effectively compare apples with apples when it comes to the various products on offer. Lenders in all states except Tasmania and Western Australia must display the AAPR, not just the advertised rate.

Your personalities may well determine your choice of loan. If you are both solid earners and savers, then a variable loan or an all-in-one option may make more sense. If one is by nature a worrier, then a fixed-rate loan or half fixed/half variable may ease the nerves and be a sensible compromise.

The following is a guide to some of the more popular loans. As I mentioned earlier, there are thousands of different types of loans. To find out more, visit the Websites of mortgage brokers listed in the panel on page 95.

Standard variable

This loan has an interest rate which fluctuates with the general level of interest rates in the economy. It will be influenced, for example, by the Reserve Bank's monetary policy settings and economic conditions generally. This can be an advantage over a fixed-rate loan if interest rates are declining. You pay off the principal and interest and most institutions have a maximum length of time in which to do so. You can also often make lump-sum payments.

Fixed

Unlike the variable loan, this has a fixed interest rate, a fixed length of time and therefore fixed amounts of repayments. This type of loan is appropriate if there is evidence that interest rates will rise, as you will be cushioned from any increases. However, you will be locked into a higher interest rate should rates fall. Also, should you wish to pay out your loan earlier than the term specified, you will find that you may be up for a penalty cost, commonly called a 'break cost'.

Combination/split

A split loan allows you to have both a fixed and a variable component. This gives you the best of both worlds if you can't decide which way to go, and cushions part of your money from potential rises in interest rates. Make sure that any 'split' or 'switching' fees do not erode the benefit of locking in a low rate.

Equity

For those couples with strong willpower who are not likely to spend up on that latest sports car, this type of loan may be ideal. Its main feature is that you borrow a set amount and have a line of credit available should you need it for a special purchase. For example, say you borrow $200 000 for an apartment and diligently pay off $50 000 within a few years. You will then be able to access that $50 000 if you want to carry out renovations, for example, or even to buy units in a managed fund. Often these types of loans do not have a set term so you need to be sensible about setting clear guidelines on how to use this facility. But you may pay, through a higher rate, for the luxury of not having to gain approval each time you want to draw down.

All-in-one

In this instance, your salary is paid directly into your home loan account, effectively reducing your loan balance (and therefore your interest) from the minute you are paid, with your living expenses then withdrawn as you require them. These accounts are a smart idea, but the main advantage derives from the extra money left in after your expenses are withdrawn—that is, the extra repayments you make with what is left over. Otherwise, the only real benefit is the short period—after your salary goes in, before your bills come out—during which interest will be charged on a lower balance. But every little bit counts. If you have to pay a premium—higher fees or a higher interest rate—for these facilities, the costs may well outweigh the benefits.

Interest-only

If you are borrowing for an investment property, this type of loan may be the most suitable. It requires you to pay the interest component for the term of the loan then the principal amount in full at the end, which is usually paid for from the sale of the property. If you wish to hang on to the property, you can simply renegotiate another loan at the end of the term.

GET HELP TO GET THE RIGHT LOAN

Shopping around for the best home loan can be tedious, emotionally draining and time-consuming. It may mean going from one financial institution to another and providing the same details over and over—on the phone, in person or on the Internet. Then, if your application is rejected, you are back to square one.

In a time-poor, high-stress society, this process may intensify the traumatic experience of buying a property. That's why mortgage brokers are gaining popularity, with about 20 per cent of consumers relying on their services to secure a home loan that hopefully offers them as much flexibility as possible at a competitive rate.

An accredited broker can save you the hassle of traipsing from one lender to another and can help you find the best deal. You simply give them your details then that broker should have access to a wide range of lenders with hundreds of products across the market.

If you're in the market for a mortgage broker, find out how they are paid. Feel free to ask exactly what their commission will be. Find out how many institutions they deal with—the more the better. Discuss how many mortgage options they will offer you. A good broker should provide you with at least two different home loan packages and be able to recommend lenders you may not have thought of approaching.

Ask as many questions as possible. Find out about loans with a redraw facility and how often you can redraw without incurring a fee, fixed versus variable rates and whether the loan is portable if you do sell to buy another property. Ask whether you can make additional repayments without penalty to help pay off your mortgage faster.

Even though it's not compulsory, you may prefer a mortgage

broker who is a member of the Mortgage Industry Association of Australia, which has a binding code of practice. If you like your broker, you can build on the relationship when adding to your property portfolio. Your details will be on record and you'll only need to update your details rather than start all over again.

To find a broker through the Mortgage Industry Association of Australia, visit:

www.miaa.com.au

Broker sites to browse:

www.austral.com.au
www.iconexhomeloans.com.au
www.mortgagestore.com.au
www.mortgagechoice.com.au
www.bmcloans.com.au
www.smartline.com.au

PAY OFF YOUR MORTGAGE FASTER

Being proud home owners is often tarnished by the burden of paying off your mortgage. For many, a 25-year loan commitment can seem like a lifetime, and paying it off can seem an impossible mission when simple pleasures in life, such as going to the movies, eating out or weekends away together, must be sacrificed.

It's no secret that paying off as much as you can will get you there faster and there are many tricks to ease the pain, including rounding up your repayments, making repayments at a higher interest rate and making 26 fortnightly repayments each year (which equates to thirteen monthly payments instead of twelve).

Other ways to bring forward your debt-free days include all-in-one loan facilities or 100 per cent offset accounts to accompany your loan (see the section on your home loan choices above). If you're disciplined, you can achieve a similar effect with an ordinary loan account—simply by taking any money remaining at the end of your pay period and depositing it into your mortgage. Check whether your mortgage allows a redraw if you need to get the extra cash out later, how many times they'll allow this and whether there is a charge each time you do so.

Don't underestimate the value of these extra payments—especially during the early years. Table 8.1 shows the monthly repayments of $1060 on a $150 000 loan at an annual interest rate of 7 per cent over 25 years. Initially, the proportion representing a repayment of the principal is low, and the proportion representing interest is high. In this example, the interest component is initially more than 80 per cent of the repayment—and this would be even higher with a higher interest rate or longer loan period.

Extra repayments reduce your principal. And a reduced principal means lower interest costs for the rest of your loan term. If you can pay extra early, it means lower interest costs start sooner. In fact, for the mortgage described above, $1000 paid in at the beginning of your mortgage can save you more than $4600 in interest costs over the life of the loan. That same extra payment made five years later will wipe about $3000 off future interest costs.

It really pays to be ahead in your repayments if you are expecting periods of reduced income or extra expenses—for example, if you plan to take time out of the workforce to raise a family of if you need to rent somewhere else to live while

Table 8.1 Monthly repayments

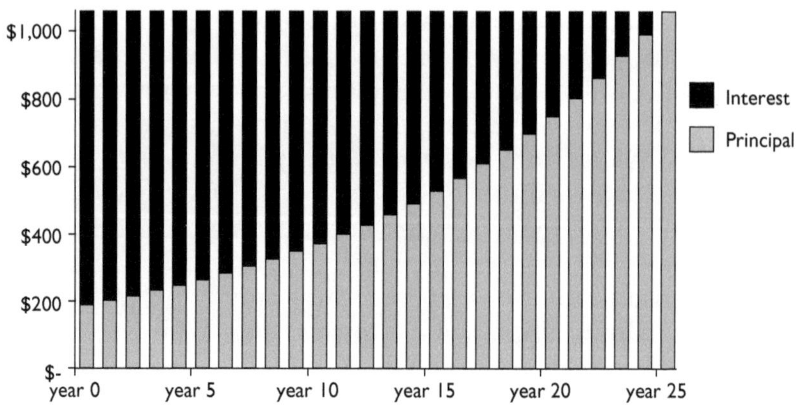

Assumptions: Loan of $150 000; 7% pa over 25 years; regular repayments of $1060.17 per month.

renovating your home. Get ahead early and you'll reap the rewards.

Lump sums, such as an inheritance or an unusually high tax refund, can be used to bring down the cost of your mortgage and bring forward your debt-free future. But seek advice first—depending on your individual circumstances, a financial adviser may suggest investing the money elsewhere or adding to your superannuation.

Of course, if you're like many other couples you'll have traded your mortgage in for a larger loan on a bigger house long before you've paid it off. Then you can look forward to doing it all over again!

YOUR DREAM HOME

You've done your sums and found the mortgage which best suits your needs. But before you open the newspaper, visit your local real estate agent or surf the Web for properties, you need to discuss the following:

- Do you want a house or an apartment? This may be determined by the maximum amount you are able to borrow on your joint income or by whether you have children or plan to have them.
- The must-have features—for example, the number of bedrooms and bathrooms, a garden, parking, views, etc.
- The features you are prepared to trade off, such as a second bathroom, a carport in place of a garage, a park view rather than a water view, a semi-detached cottage instead of a free-standing one, a renovated rather than unrenovated place, a garden instead of a courtyard, a modern or older style.
- Will the purchase be a long-term investment or just a stepping stone to something bigger down the track?
- Do you want to live close to town or in the suburbs?
- Limiting your search to two or three suburbs then widening it as you have more idea of what you want and what you can afford.
- If you don't have the time, employ a professionally qualified

property consultant (see the *Yellow Pages*) who will do the legwork for you and present you with a short list of properties to view. They can also represent you throughout the buying process if you choose. While these experts cost money, they can save you from having to give up your precious Saturdays for the next six months!

- Attend a few auctions so you understand the process. Often, agents will under-value a property just to get more people along to a sale.
- Keep in mind the resale value. You may believe that this is your dream home and you will never want to budge. But you never know . . .
- Attractions such as good access to public transport, schools and shopping centres rarely go out of fashion. Also, if other houses in the area are in various stages of renovation, this can be a good sign that other people have identified the locality for its growth potential.
- If you are keen on an area but have never lived there, consider renting for six months to find out what it is like and whether it suits you.

RESEARCH, RESEARCH, RESEARCH

Property is not just about location, location, location. It's about research, research, research. Be prepared to spend a great deal of time looking for the right property. I can't stress enough the importance of doing your homework. Remember to look beyond the existing house and its décor. Consider its potential, but also think about how much it will cost to renovate—beware of underestimating! Ultimately, the value of your investment depends on the location itself and its ability to be further capitalised . . . but not overcapitalised. As I've said before, this will probably be the biggest investment you both make, so you want to devote plenty of time to the cause, keep your emotions in check and remember that if you miss out on what you think is your dream home there is always another one around the corner. Time spent on research means visiting as many properties as you can, attending auctions and keeping track of values in the areas of your choice. Then you will be in a position to know when you should buy.

BEFORE YOU BUY

Register your names and requirements with estate agents and ask them to let you know if they have a match. Regularly check the local and daily newspapers and Internet sites devoted to selling properties. Once you have narrowed your search, check out the property midweek, in the evenings and at weekends to see whether it suffers from too much noise. Talk to neighbours and visit local shops and parks to check whether it will meet your needs.

Websites such as www.homepriceguide.com.au can provide information on sales in your chosen areas for the previous twelve months to give you a guide on how much you should pay. This service costs about $50 to search for sales in any particular postcode and is available in all states of Australia except for Tasmania and the Northern Territory.

Before you decide to buy, have the property inspected by a registered builder or architect to ensure there are no building defects. You may choose to ask a family friend with building experience or enlist the help of experts such as Archicentre (www.archicentre.com.au). For a fee, this organisation will provide a written report on the state of the property including any water problems, structural defects and termite or white ant damage. This is particularly important if you are buying an older home that may have been touched up with a quick coat of paint to hide serious problems.

If you are buying an apartment, make sure your conveyancer or solicitor has a report done on the records of the body corporate or company to check its financial health, any upcoming works that may require levies and details of any recent disputes.

BEFORE THE AUCTION

At auctions, be aware that thrillseeker types will probably pay anything to secure the property while timid may struggle to make a bid. Steady won't pay a cent more than they can afford while savvy will pay above the odds if it's a good deal.

For the sake of your finances and your relationship, make sure you have agreed on what you can afford and are willing to pay *before* the auction, and make a resolution not to get emotionally involved and go over this limit.

AT THE AUCTION

Your heart is pumping wildly and the hammer goes down. Suddenly, the property is yours. As well as elation, the enormity of your purchase will start to hit home.

If your final bid is accepted, you are legally bound to purchase the property. You must pay an immediate non-refundable deposit of 10 per cent and contracts of sale will be signed and exchanged on the day. Therefore, it is imperative to have your finances sorted out and your loan approved by your preferred lender before you bid. If you subsequently decide not to go ahead with the purchase, you will probably lose your 10 per cent deposit. It's a hefty price to pay for losing your head at an auction!

MAKE AN OFFER

If the property is being offered for sale, this process can be the most nerve-wracking of all, particularly if you have your heart set on a place and you just want to offer what the vendor is asking. However, it is important not to let your emotions run away with you, as you could end up paying more than the property is worth. You both need to agree on your upper limit and not be tempted to exceed that amount without consulting each other.

Usually, you should first offer an amount lower than the vendor's asking price. The estate agent acting on behalf of the vendor is then required to submit your offer for consideration. Sometimes your offer may have a time or date limit attached and may also be conditional on items such as built-in appliances or garden fixtures remaining in or with the house.

The most common procedure is that once the vendor has accepted your offer, both parties need to sign a contract containing all details of the property, how much is being paid, what the deposit is and the settlement terms. A vendor is not legally bound to your offer until they too have signed the contract. Until that time, the vendor can still accept other offers, even though you have signed the contract.

Most contracts also have a 'cooling off' period (normally five days) unless this has been waived by both parties. This means that, should either party change their mind during that period, the deal does not go ahead. Check out the contract—you could lose up to 0.25 per cent of your deposit if you get cold feet.

LEGAL AFFAIRS

The legal side of buying a property involves removing one set of names from title documents and inserting a new set. When it comes to conveyancing, the process where property ownership is lawfully passed to another, you have the choice of using either a professional conveyancer, a solicitor or a do-it-yourself kit.

If you have been building a relationship with a solicitor for some years, you may prefer to choose this option, as you may feel more comfortable with the level of knowledge and service. Just make sure that the firm is not too tied up with court matters to return phone calls and complete the required paperwork on time.

Conveyancers consider themselves property law professionals because they specialise in just this one aspect of the law. For that reason, they are not tied up in court, which means they should be available to a client at all times. Conveyancers are normally no more expensive than a solicitor, usually charging a flat rate of $600 to $900 if you are selling a property. If you are buying, expect to pay $800 to $1200. Whichever option you choose, make sure you ask about the fees they charge.

If you have had some experience with conveyancing, you may wish to consider a DIY kit, which can be found either on the Internet or in the Yellow Pages under 'Conveyancing services'.

For the uninitiated, it may not be wise to take short cuts with such a big investment. Legal language can be confusing, contracts can be time-consuming and if you make a mistake you are responsible. For example, it is easy to miss information in a title search. If you do not know what you are looking for, you may find yourself buying a property zoned partly residential/ partly commercial, or that the person named in the contract as the vendor does not actually own the property.

WHAT IF YOUR PARTNER ALREADY HAS A MORTGAGE?

If one partner already has a mortgage and the other starts contributing to the payments, an agreement can be drawn up between the two of you to outline each person's share. This should be done through a solicitor. Of course, it is advisable to keep good financial records in case you decide to change the arrangement or it ends up being tested in court.

If you wish to buy into the mortgage and you want your name added to the title, you will need the lender's consent. A new mortgage would have to be issued, with the associated paperwork and costs. If you are married, no stamp duty is payable on the transfer of ownership to joint names if it is your permanent place of residence. Same sex and de facto couples should check their respective state laws.

TENANTS IN COMMON/JOINT TENANTS

If you are buying a property together, you must decide whether to do it as joint tenants or tenants in common. Joint tenants own equal shares. If one partner dies, then the surviving joint tenant automatically gets the other share. In the case of tenants in common, if one partner dies, their will determines who gets their share of the property. This may be more suitable if you are buying a property with friends or in a syndicate.

INVESTMENT PROPERTY

Before you buy an investment property, you need to research the market just as thoroughly as you would when buying your own home. There are certain times when it is madness to even consider such a move—for example, when there is a glut of rental properties or when property prices are so high that you will be unable to generate the required rental return as seen in recent years.

The main reason people buy an investment property is for capital growth and the tax benefits available through negative gearing, which comes into play when the interest and associated expenses on the loan to buy an investment are greater than the income generated. You can then claim any shortfall as a tax deduction against other income (there will be no benefit if you don't earn other income, as in the case of a non-working spouse). In the case of an investment property, you can also claim repairs (but not improvements), agents' fees, maintenance, insurance and depreciation (on carpets, curtains, etc.).

Before buying, you need to decide whose name should be on the title. Should it be in his, her or joint names? This may depend on who most needs the tax benefit. If in doubt, seek advice from a qualified financial planner. If your partner is in the top tax bracket, the property may be better in his or her name to reap the most benefits.

When buying the investment property, you need to apply many of the same principles as you would when buying your own home: have your deposit and additional funds to meet unexpected costs such as maintenance; do your research; choose an attractive location close to amenities and public transport; and find the right loan. But there are some other key issues you should consider.

- Your aim should be for a solid, positive, long-term capital gain.
- The property should be in an area that will generate a good rental return, such as near a shopping centre, beach, parks, etc.
- If the property doesn't increase in value more than the accumulated loss in rent and interest, you can lose money.
- In times of low inflation, be prepared for rental returns as low as 2–5 per cent.
- If buying an apartment, you may have to fork out funds for special levies—for example, painting, concrete cancer, rising damp, etc.

- If buying a house, there will be ongoing maintenance costs.
- Factor in the possibility that the property may be vacant for between four and eight weeks of the year in between tenants.
- Consider the costs of advertising for tenants and agents' management fees, then factor those in.
- If buying an apartment, be prepared to attend body corporate meetings to keep up to date with issues and to have a say in any proposed capital works.

OFF THE PLAN

If you are interested in purchasing an investment property, then it may be worth consider buying off the plan. This basically means that you agree to buy a property before it has been constructed based on design plans and a model provided by the developer. Among the advantages are that you don't have to pay the full purchase price until work is finished on the property, which may be months or even years later, and you are buying at today's prices rather than tomorrow's. Remember that, depending on the property market, your investment may be worth more *or* less tomorrow than it is today, particularly in the inner-city apartment market.

You need to be aware of how the rental market is performing and whether you will easily find a tenant after the property is completed. If your aim is to make a capital gain on or before completion, you need to get your timing right and be confident that the market is going to move in your favour. Also, you would be wise to find out about the reputation of the builder, the quality of fittings and whether the display apartment mirrors the property you are buying—for example, whether the ceiling height matches the dimensions in your floorplan. Make sure you have your solicitor or conveyancer look at the contract, as it may permit changes to fittings or even layout.

DEPOSIT BONDS

Some people buying an off-the-plan property are turning to deposit bonds as a way to finance the purchase if they don't want to use their own capital or don't have the cash. Amateur investors need to consider this strategy long and hard and should not be swayed by get-rich sales talk.

It can be a cheap alternative, generally only costing around 0.35 per cent of the purchase price for a settlement within twelve months, or more for a longer settlement. For example, if the property is worth $500 000, instead of having to fork out $50 000 for the required deposit, you can buy a twelve-month deposit bond for around $1750 and still have the $50 000 tucked away in your bank account.

The company issuing the bond guarantees that a deposit is paid to the vendor even if the deal falls through. Of course, the defaulting purchaser will still be liable for the amount of the bond if they cannot on-sell or find the finance. The major issuers of bonds are Royal & SunAlliance, GE Mortgage Insurance Services and QBE. Check with the developer to make sure they accept this form of deposit. In a hot property market, some investors use this option as a cheap means of securing a deposit on an off-the-plan apartment then onselling the property for a profit before settlement. Be aware that if the property market moves against you, you could be faced with having to find finance on a property that has reduced in value.

RENTING VERSUS BUYING

When the housing market is overheated and there is a glut of rental properties and the threat of rising interest rates, this is the time to seriously consider the merits of renting versus buying.

Sure, all the experts will tell you that you can't go past owning your own home as a long-term investment. But will it be your dream home or will it simply be a way of sampling the great Australian love affair with bricks and mortar? Will the decision to buy mean a totally different lifestyle?

Take a couple who were renting a two-bedroom inner-city apartment in Melbourne with water views and a northerly aspect. They walked to work, restaurants, cinemas and theatre. There was no garden to maintain apart from half a dozen plants on their balcony. All their friends lived within 10 kilometres so they had an active social life.

Their rent was affordable and had barely changed in their five years of living together. This meant they were able to stack away some savings, with the long-term goal of saving for a house deposit.

When they had amassed enough for a 20 per cent deposit, they embarked on the house-hunting trail. Every Saturday morning, they would head off to look at properties listed in their local newspaper and armed with printouts from real estate Websites.

They started off in the leafy suburb where they were renting. But after attending a few auctions, they realised the prices were out of the question. So they moved a few suburbs away. Same story. The only option was to head further afield, away from friends and the lifestyle they loved.

Even though they felt under pressure to be part of the brick owners' brigade, they quickly realised they would miss their easy-going lifestyle. Just to be sure, they made a list of all the pros of renting.

- They could rent in a suburb they couldn't afford to buy in.
- They had plenty of leisure time.
- They had a lovely view and aspect.
- They could move at any time.
- They did not have to commute to work.
- If they did break up, there would be no messy property division.
- They had no maintenance costs and no levies.
- They had more flexibility, especially if they had to move to further their careers.
- They were not fixed to a mortgage so not concerned about rising interest rates.
- They did not have to spend their weekends mowing lawns, visiting nurseries or doing repairs.
- As their rent had not risen for some time, they had more disposable income, which they could invest in the sharemarket.

Then they made another list on the pros of buying a home.

- They would have a slice of the valuable property market.
- It would mean putting money into a growth asset.

- It would be the biggest investment they would ever make.
- It would be free of capital gains tax.
- They would not be at the whim of landlords.
- They could renovate to their own taste.
- They would have an emotional and financial attachment.
- They would be paying off their own mortgage, not someone else's.
- Inflation would chisel away at a home loan but would only increase their rent.
- It would be a form of forced saving.
- Long-term, they should come out in front financially.

After weighing up both lists, they decided to stay in their rented apartment and enjoy their lifestyle until the property market steadied in response to rising interest rates.

Buying a home needs to make sense according to the economics of the time. If the market is overheated, it might be more sensible to put your money elsewhere and wait for it to cool down. As all the property experts say: 'Buy in the lulls and sell in the boom times!'.

BUYING VERSUS RENOVATING

One way of increasing the value of your property is to renovate. This is particularly effective if you are thinking of moving due to lack of space and haven't considered putting on an extra storey or increasing the size of your living areas.

A word of caution, though. The biggest risk with renovations is over-capitalisation—that is, when the cost of your renovations is greater than the market value they add to your home. You may spend $150 000 adding a second storey, but when you come to sell you may not be able to recoup the outlay. The choice is to take a loss or wait until inflation raises market values. Neither is a good option.

Despite this, there is no doubt that a wise renovation can add value to your home. All the experts agree that you can increase value by renovating kitchens and bathrooms, adding an ensuite or extra bathroom, providing an entertainment area and family room, installing appropriate floor coverings, built-ins and lighting, even tidying gardens and painting in neutral shades.

Just don't go overboard by adding a second storey, swimming pool, spa, designer appliances and fittings and a high-maintenance garden if you're not sure you can recoup your cost.

Potential buyers look closely at kitchens and bathrooms, and the ratio of bathrooms to bedrooms. The backyard is another area where you can add real value, especially if you have a family room opening on to a courtyard or garden.

Speaking from my own experience, the one area where people over-capitalise is in the fittings. There is little use in buying the most expensive taps, door handles and light fittings when the only people who will appreciate them will be you! These can also add thousands of dollars to your final bill so be conservative in your choices.

Before renovating, seek advice from a few real estate agents in your area who should be able to tell you whether or not you will be over-capitalising. Attend a few open houses and watch how the market reacts to gauge what's working and what's not. Then set a budget and make sure you stick to it.

Before drawing up your plans, you need to consider the type of person who will buy the home—even if you're not planning to sell for another five years or so.

If you have a small apartment, save some dollars by buying in bulk and tiling the kitchen and bathroom in the same tiles. You can also save on space by putting a washing machine in the kitchen under the bench space or in the bathroom.

By keeping walls a neutral colour, you can brighten up rooms with different shades in furnishings. Or you can do feature walls in blocks of colour, which can be painted over easily by the new owners. If you don't want to spend too much on the actual property, spend it on furniture and paintings instead to enhance the home—then you can take them with you when you leave.

It's generally the kitchen where renovators lose control. Try not to be enticed by that expensive Italian marble benchtop which will end up costing you more than the whole kitchen.

There are many options that look fabulous but don't cost a fortune. For example, cupboards can be enhanced by a fresh coat of paint and some plain stainless-steel handles.

If it's a family home, keep a flat, grassy space where children can play and a paved area for entertaining. If you have an inner-city terrace, make the most of a courtyard so that people can dine outdoors. By the time you have finished renovating, you may well have put the idea of moving house out of your mind!

LISTED PROPERTY TRUSTS

It's estimated that more than three million people have taken the opportunity to diversify into another form of property investment called listed property trusts (LPTs). These are entities listed on the Australian Stock Exchange which own, manage and develop real estate, including large office blocks in CBDs, big shopping centres, industrial warehouses, hotels and residential properties.

LPTs own a total of $65 billion in property assets, mainly in Australia, New Zealand and the United States. And, just as corporate Australia has been expanding offshore, so too have LPTs. 'In 1996, 100 per cent of all LPT assets were in Australia, but today some 29 per cent of underlying assets are in offshore markets,' says property expert Stuart Stuckey. 'This puts forward some interesting opportunities for investors.'

In the past decade, LPTs have been a strong performing asset class.

Stuckey cites the following as some of the key advantages of LPTs:

- They give investors a chance to access all the different types of real estate assets—office, retail, industrial and hotel—both domestically and internationally.
- They give people who like real estate a chance to diversify away from the residential market. There is nothing wrong with residential real estate but it does tend to form such a substantial component of our investment base, arguably too

high an amount. Property trusts can allow you to access these opportunities in other real estate markets with minimal capital.

- The trusts also offer liquidity. They are traded on the stock exchange so investors can buy and sell swiftly through a broker. If you have ever bought or sold a residential or investment property, you will be well aware of how long it can take.
- LPT units are free of stamp duty but the trusts still incur stamp duty costs on their property transactions. In contrast, stamp duty on residential property varies around the country but is around 5 per cent.
- You can buy in small parcels—say, a few hundred dollars at a time—which is something you can't do with other forms of real estate.
- The average yield as of 30 June 2003 was about 7.5 per cent—after deductions for professional management fees. However, you need to be aware that it is the yield rather than the capital growth that makes LPTs attractive. This may not suit people who are at the higher end of the risk spectrum and in search of much more substantial capital growth.
- There are tax credits associated with the income from distributions from LPTs, which may mean you don't pay full tax.
- A team of professionals manages the assets and takes care of key components of the real estate business: leasing, management, acquisition and development. It's similar to what your local real estate agent does but on a much bigger scale. This means you don't have to worry about when or how to buy, sell, finance, upgrade, re-lease, refurbish or manage property. It's all taken care of for you.
- You can invest directly through a broker or indirectly through a managed fund.
- Transaction costs are negligible relative to buying and selling a property.
- Some LPTs own up to 100 assets so there is plenty of diversification across different classes of property.

Jane and Steven have been saving hard to buy a house for the past ten years. They have a combined income of $85 000, pay $500 a week in rent and have accumulated $65 000 in savings after selling their second car and cutting back on holidays and dining out. They have no debts and pay off the balance of their $3000 limit credit card every month. And yes, they are both steady personalities!

They feel like they are in a position to buy a home and have their heart set on a $450 000 property on the New South Wales–Queensland border that is part of a new housing estate. Yet they really have no idea how much they can borrow.

If Jane and Steven were to put down a 10 per cent deposit of $45 000 on their $450 000 home, they would need to borrow $405 000. Their stamp duty on the property would be about $15 740 and stamp duty on the mortgage of about $1560 ($146 for the first $50 000 then $4 per thousand thereafter).

If the couple were to take out a standard variable loan at 6.32 per cent, their minimum monthly repayments would be $2690 a month over 25 years. At the moment, they are paying $2166 a month in rent so they will need to find about an extra $500 a month.

As neither has ever owned property, they are also eligible for the federal government's $7000 first home owner's grant. As Jane and Steven will be borrowing more than 80 per cent of the property's value, they will also have to fork out up to $5900 for lender's mortgage insurance. Then there are legal fees, which can range from $1000 to $2500—plus the standard bank application fee of between $600 and $1000, home building insurance and pest and building inspection costs. Ideally, before they buy, this means they will need about $71 000. With their savings of $65 000, they can make up the shortfall using their $7000 grant.

The good news for Jane and Steven is that they should be in a position to be offered a loan by financial institutions because they have a solid employment record, a good credit track record, are proven savers with no debts and have a 10 per cent deposit. What banks will normally do is assess clients at a higher rate than the standard variable to test their serviceability if interest rates do rise. Given their income and savings, Jane and Steven should pass this test.

The couple can also show evidence that they pay off their credit card each month. But if you cannot show that you have paid off the past six statements in full, the bank will take up to 5 per cent of your credit card limit into account as a monthly commitment. However, Jane and Steven will need to revisit their budget to meet the extra $500 a month.

The don'ts of property investing

- Don't lose your head at auctions and pay more than you can afford.
- Don't buy in boom times (if you can avoid it).
- Don't get emotionally attached.
- Don't be swayed by good or bad furnishings.
- Don't swallow your agent's hard sell.
- Don't buy without a building inspection.
- Don't sell when the market has fallen (if you can avoid it).

Your home-buying team

Mortgage broker
Conveyancing agent/solicitor
Building inspector
Pest controller
Architect (if necessary)
Financial planner
Accountant (particularly if an investment property)
A trusted second opinion

What is a redraw facility?

With a redraw facility, if you have already made additional payments on your loan to reduce the principal, you can then redraw these funds at any time should you need them. The facility allows you to place extra earnings against your home loan, reducing the interest you pay each month.

What options are there if the banks won't lend us money?

A new breed of financial institutions called non-conforming lenders are becoming popular. They usually lend to self-employed, casual workers, or those with a blemished credit rating or inadequate savings history. Admittedly, they charge higher rates due to the increased risk. However, the size of the market means more players are entering, providing increased competition on interest rates. Traditional lenders are also offering these products, known as 'LoDoc' loans.

9

How to make loads from a little

Myth: We have to be wealthy to be investors.
Fact: We have to be investors to be wealthy.

Couples all over the world have always been attracted to 'get-rich-quick schemes'. But, aside from a lucky lotto win, there is rarely such a thing. If you talk to any wealthy couple, they will more than likely say that the key to creating wealth is determination, discipline and perseverance.

Sounds boring, doesn't it. The problem is that, after paying for the mortgage, the car, insurance premiums, medical bills and credit card debts, there is usually not much—if anything—left over. Does this sound like your household?

Yet an essential step in achieving long-term financial success as a couple is to free up your income to invest as soon as you can. This is often the most difficult step, as there always seem to be more bills to be paid and unexpected outlays. But once you have set out your goals and done your budget, freeing up those initial dollars will be a liberating experience. Once you see the power of saving, you will be hooked. However, you need to clear your debts first. I'm not talking about your mortgage here; I'm talking about debts such as credit cards and hire purchase arrangements. See Chapter 5 for guidance on budgeting.

The next vital move in achieving financial success is making sound investment choices. While this may sound simple, there are some fundamental points to note before you plunge headlong into the investment market.

WHAT ARE OUR CHOICES FOR INVESTING?

Investing brings with it a multitude of options—listed shares, managed funds, fixed interest, cash management products and so on. Aside from property, which was dealt with in Chapter 8, the following are the most common vehicles in which to invest your money, along with a guide to when it may be most appropriate.

Cash

The most common types of cash investment are bank savings accounts, cash management trusts and fixed term deposits. These types of investment vehicles are all known as short-term investments. They are relatively secure as they invest predominantly in the short-term money market.

Money markets facilitate the transfer of cash between borrowers and lenders. The short-term money market invests primarily in short-term money and short-term securities—for example, bills of exchange and certificates of deposit. As a result, the risk of losing is remote but your returns will suffer. These products barely beat inflation, so leave your money here indefinitely and it may well decrease in value in real (inflation adjusted) terms.

Will this suit us?

If you want to park your money for a short period because you are waiting to buy a property or shares, or you simply want to have ready access to some cash, this type of investment vehicle may suit you. But remember, it won't make you rich.

Fixed interest

The term fixed interest quite simply means that you agree to lend your funds to the institution, whether it be the government, a bank or a company, and that in return they agree to make regular interest payments known as 'coupons' throughout this period, and to repay the principal at a predetermined date. The amount of the coupons is 'fixed'. Types of fixed interest investments include:

- *Term deposits*. These are the more traditional type of fixed interest investments and are issued by banks and credit unions. The terms are generally anywhere between one or two months and five years. As a general rule, the longer the period, the higher the rate.
- *Bonds*. A bond issuer is normally a government, bank or a company wanting to borrow money. A bond holder has the security of knowing they will receive regular income from the coupon payments, as well as the return of their capital at the end of the period. However, this also will depend on the strength of the company the bond was purchased from. Government and semi-government bonds are seen as the most secure and have the strongest credit rating, which typically means they pay the lowest interest rate. You may have heard television newsreaders talk about bond prices rising or the bond market rallying. That means when the general level of interest rates in the economy falls, the price of a bond on the secondary market rises because its higher 'coupon' rate is more valuable—thus the saying 'the bond markets rallied'.
- *Debentures*. These are offered by finance companies—the security of these will depend on the financial strength of the company issuing them.
- *Unsecured notes*. They are issued by finance companies and other corporations as a means of borrowing money. However, as they are unsecured, they are generally seen as more risky, which is why you will often receive a higher interest rate.

Will this suit us?

Unlike buying shares in a company where you reap the rewards if the company is successful, what you see is what you get when buying a fixed interest investment. You will not participate in the rise or fall of the share price but you will generally be safe in the knowledge that you will get your money back when the period is completed. Of course, except for government and semi-government bonds, this will depend on the stability and strength of the company issuing them. Fixed interest is a sensible option if you have also bought shares and property and want to round out your portfolio.

Shares

Also known as stocks or equities, shares represent ownership of a part of a company. When you buy a share in a company, you become a joint owner of the business and share in its profits—and losses. Shares are generally known to have the highest growth potential of all investment types, provided you take a long-term view.

As well as providing capital growth when the value of the share price rises, shares can provide regular income through the payments of dividends. This is because, when companies make a profit, they have a choice of what to do with the funds.

They can pay some or all of the profit to shareholders as a dividend payment, they can buy back their own shares, or they can reinvest the profit back into the company—for example, to finance expansion, new technologies or equipment. This ability to reinvest to foster greater growth and profits can result in higher share prices—the benefits of which are passed on to shareholders.

Often, a company will choose to divide its profit and pay a portion as dividends to shareholders then reinvest the remainder back into the company. Ultimately, the shareholders can receive the twofold benefit of regular dividend payments, as well as greater growth in share prices in the longer term.

Investing in Australian shares can provide yet another benefit in the form of dividend imputation. This means that if a company has paid tax on its profits and distributes these profits to shareholders as dividends, the shareholders who are residents for Australian tax purposes get a credit against their tax equal to the amount of tax already paid by the company on their share of the profit. The same rules apply if you invest in shares through a managed investment. This means that an Australian share fund can provide a tax-efficient income stream as well as capital growth over time.

Will this suit us?

Investing in listed shares is good for couples who are interested in the share market—and have time to do the research—or are happy to let a stockbroker select stocks. Inevitably, you will need to watch your portfolio to be ready to buy or sell when the time suits. This type of investing will require time and patience, and the knowledge to keep a finger on the stock market pulse. Shares are discussed further in Chapter 10.

MANAGED FUNDS

If you don't have the time, energy or skill to choose your own investment products, then managed funds may be for you. Here your money is pooled with a large group of investors, providing access to a wider range of investments. But there are many other benefits.

- You can start with as little as $1000. For many funds, minimum amounts range from $1000 to $5000. If you have, say, $20 000 to invest, you could place $10 000 in two funds or spread your money across four funds with $5000 in each. There are entry fees to consider, which can range from 0 to 5 per cent of your initial investment. These may vary if you use the services of a financial adviser, who may also charge a fee. Some funds charge exit fees, depending on when you withdraw your money. Management fees vary from 0.5 to 2 per cent of the value of your account balance. Check all the details before you make a commitment.
- Managed funds are monitored by professionals with access to the most up-to-date research. Before investing, check a manager's credentials and track record, focusing on long-term performance. Has the investment team been a strong performer? Has it been stable? What is their investment style? How do they manage risk in the portfolio?
- Managed funds generally offer a relatively attractive and convenient way of opening up new investment options to the average investor. For example, they invest in assets like shares and property and, for that reason, should deliver a better rate of return than your standard savings bank account over the long term. But you should also expect short-term volatility, especially after a crisis of investment confidence

like that which followed the September 11 terrorist attacks in the United States in 2001.

- Managed funds can help reduce your risk. With access to a wide range of investments and asset classes—for example, shares (Australian and international), cash, fixed interest and property—you can choose to invest across a broad range of sectors via a balanced diversified fund or focus on areas such as small companies, Australian shares, ethical investments or emerging markets. You can also diversify into funds that invest internationally, or in commercial properties. These sectors are not always accessible to direct investors. Discovering your appetite for risk and understanding your risk profiles will help you with your decision. For example, if you are young, or have a longer investment time frame, you may be happier to go for a higher growth, more volatile asset class. If you always worry about money, you may be suited to more conservative investments.
- Managed funds provide a disciplined way to save. Many funds offer the facility to make regular payments via a direct debit from your salary or bank account. This can be as little as $100 a month. Using a direct debit will boost your balance, you may not even notice the regular withdrawal and you won't be able to spend it before it can be invested. If your circumstances change, you can simply suspend deposits or vary the amount. By using a direct debit or 'easy investment plan', you can take advantage of dollar-cost averaging, where you automatically buy more units when the market is down and fewer when it is up. Some funds provide an income distribution to unit holders, generally quarterly, half-yearly or annually. The distribution can be paid in cash or reinvested as additional units in the fund.

Will this suit us?

Managed funds are used widely by people of all ages and risk profiles because they take the pain and stress out of choosing stocks. They also provide access to markets around the world that are difficult for direct investors to access, as well as giving access to fixed interest, property and Australian and international shares—all in the one fund. Most fund managers have products that cater to all types of investors—from timid to thrillseeker. It's a matter of finding the right one for you both. Be prepared for fluctuations in performance with the rise and fall of the stockmarket. Best results are usually achieved if you take a long-term view.

ETHICAL FUNDS

If you as a couple are concerned about the environment, human rights and abolishing uranium mining, ethical funds may be for you. Socially responsible investments (SRIs) are fast becoming popular with investors who care about the ethics of their investment impact.

SRIs work in the same way as traditional managed funds—with a small difference. A screening is applied to the choices of stocks to ensure that they comply with a fund's specific criteria. Some may avoid investing in companies involved in alcohol, tobacco, gambling or uranium mining, while others may rely on selecting the best companies in each sector rated on environmental and social performance.

The difficulty can sometimes lie in differences of interpretation. For example, you may disagree with any form of contraception and therefore believe that investing in a company that manufactures condoms is unacceptable. The fund, on the other hand, may not have a problem with this. If you are particularly keen to know exactly what screening is used for an ethical fund, it is best to check with a fund manager before making your decision.

Will this suit us?

As with all managed funds, returns vary. Some experts say that the opportunity to create good returns is minimised due to the strict selection criteria. Others say that this very issue forces fund managers to concentrate their efforts on a smaller number of stocks, which makes for a more focused product. Once again, make sure you do your research. Like any product, you will find there will be a wide range of performers so apply the same investment rules—a good track record, sound profit prospects, reputable organisation, and so on.

EMERGING MARKETS

Emerging markets are the economies of what used to be referred to as developing countries, or less developed economies.

Better economic management in some of these countries, combined with trade liberalisation and deregulation, and development of their financial systems and economies generally, has opened up many new investment opportunities—both for equity and fixed income investors.

Investing in emerging markets is a good deal more risky and volatile than investing in most industrialised or 'First World' economies. 'Country risk'—the risk of a major macroeconomic or political upheaval—is often greater, markets are thinner and the quality of information is more varied.

Will this suit us?

Emerging market investments can play a role in the context of a diversified portfolio, but beware of a large exposure. This is also an area where you are likely to be much better off relying on a specialist money manager through a well-established managed fund than attempting to do it yourself.

MASTER TRUSTS

The basic concept of a master trust is quite simple. Your cash and/or investment portfolio is pooled in a trust, which in turn invests in wholesale funds.

There are two types of master trusts: discretionary and non-discretionary. A non-discretionary trust is where you choose your strategy and the investment choices but the fund managers are chosen for you. Your portfolio is reviewed and re-weighted by the master trust manager so you are relieved of any decisions.

A discretionary master trust is the same concept except that you are able to select the managed funds you want. This is particularly attractive to people who want to exercise greater control over their investment choices and who do not want to leave these decisions to someone else.

Costs of master trusts have come down over the years and are generally in line with investing directly with retail fund managers. One benefit is that all reporting is consolidated into one report, making it easier to review your portfolio at a glance.

Will this suit us?

For those couples who want all their investments in the one spot and with one statement, master trusts and wrap accounts (see next section) may be a good option, although you generally need substantial funds to make them worthwhile.

WRAP ACCOUNTS

A wrap service literally 'wraps' around your portfolio, whether general investments or superannuation, offering an all-in-one administration, transaction and reporting service. Wrap services are also tax-deductible, so they appeal to investors on the highest marginal tax rate. The service is only available online and is typically used in conjunction with your financial adviser.

The main difference between master trusts and a wrap service is that, unlike master trusts, wraps allow investors to retain beneficial ownership of their asset. Wholesale managed funds and equities can be transferred in and out of the account without capital gains tax consequences, providing greater flexibility for advisers and their clients. This is generally not the case with a master trust.

Will this suit us?

At this stage, wraps are more suited to savvy investors on the highest marginal tax rate who demand control, flexibility, choice, portability and the latest investment tracking technology. If you have complex investments and plan to go travelling for some time, wraps can reduce the need to have someone sort through your paperwork.

TEN TIPS FOR SMART INVESTING

1 Start now and stay invested

There are always a million and one reasons to put off making investment decisions. The markets are too volatile. You want to save a little more. Your partner's birthday is next month. Christmas is around the corner.

Excuses are fine, but they won't make you rich. If you have completed a thorough budget plan, then you have hopefully freed up some cash to invest. Remember, some managed funds take as little as $1000 as an initial investment.

This decision should not be put off. If you do, you will find that five or ten years have passed and you will be sorry you didn't act sooner. You will be amazed at what a difference a few years can make to your investment proceeds if you act now.

Let's take Julie and Pete and their best friends Chloe and Tina as an example. Julie and Pete were both 32 when they moved in together after five years of dating. They knew how important it was to start investing early and were well aware of the power of two when it came to making money. They decided on an initial investment of $1000, then $100 a month into a managed fund earning an attractive 8 per cent per annum.

Compare them with Chloe and Tina, who unfortunately delayed their decision to invest because they just couldn't get their act together. Finally, when Tina was complaining about never having any money, they sat down and worked out a budget. Realising they could afford a few hundred dollars a month, they invested in the same managed fund as their friends, but starting three years later.

The good news for Julie and Pete is that, after investing a total of $13 000 over ten years, their investment is now worth $20 171. On the other hand, because they delayed their decision, Chloe and Tina's investment is worth only $12 808.

2 The power of compound interest

Albert Einstein called it the most powerful force in the universe and J.D. Rockefeller named it the eighth wonder of the world.

By simply reinvesting dividends from shares in either listed stocks or managed funds, your money works for you even harder.

Look at Figure 9.1. The compound interest is shown in the white section of the bars on the graph. Thankfully, both couples reinvested all their income over the period they were investing. But look at the end result. In the ten-year period, Julie and Pete earned compound interest of $7131. However, because Chloe and Tina delayed their decision for another three years, they earned only $3408—less than half as much.

And the longer you invest, the greater the difference in compound interest. Starting three years later meant that Chloe and

Figure 9.1 Start investing now and take advantage of compound interest

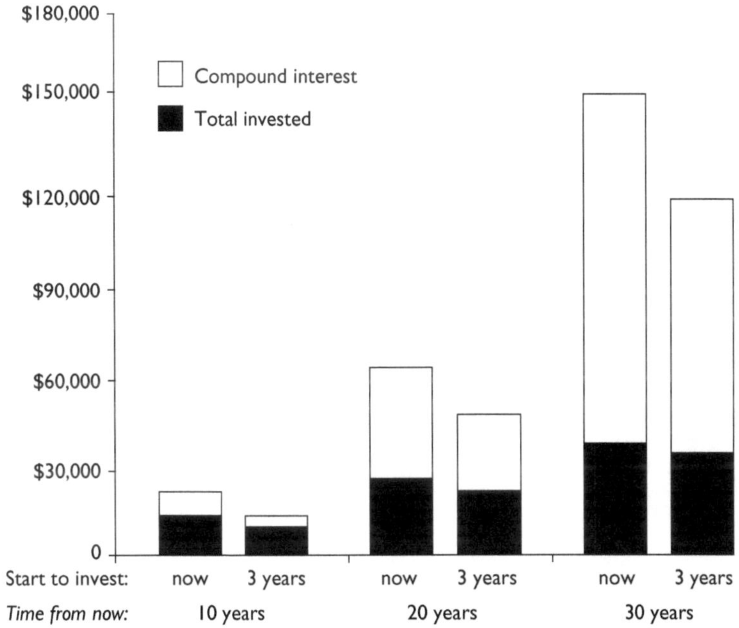

Assumptions: Initial $1000 then $100 a month. Return 8% pa compounded monthly. No allowance for inflation.

Source: BT Online Website.

Tina missed out on more than $30 000 in compound interest over 30 years.

3 Don't panic in volatile markets

This is the most common mistake that investors make. We have all seen it. The markets take a dive and splashed across the front pages of every newspaper are frightening headlines: 'Markets plunge', 'Shares crash!'. Your partner is urging you to sell your holdings and move to cash. Sure, it's difficult to sit tight when it seems like the world's stockmarkets are falling down around you. But selling your shares when the market has already fallen is like selling your house when the property market plunges—think seriously before you do it.

Many people say that it is dangerous to invest in shares when there is a market crash. In fact, it is only dangerous if you panic and sell. Even if you want to bail out, it's impossible for even the experts to predict when to buy or sell if the markets are jumping around. Think back to what your investment goals were and try to remain focused. Imagine if you sold precisely when the market bounced back! It's amazing the difference a few days of trading can make to your overall return.

4 It's not timing the market, it's time in the market

Even the professionals can't always predict when to get in and when to get out of the market. In fact, if you try to predict the market and sell out, you will need a lot of luck on your side to know exactly the best day to sell. In a ten-year period, to miss only the ten best days in trading would have meant missing out on 50 per cent of the profits during that time, according to the S&P 500 index in the United States (see Table 9.1). Sobering stuff.

5 Markets recover, eventually

After each big crisis, the market eventually manages to find its way back to positive territory, as Figure 9.2 on page 126 shows. Remember, shares are a long-term investment. As long as you

Table 9.1 Missing a few good days makes a big difference . . .

All 2608 trading days	9.27%
Minus 10 best days	4.66%
Minus 20 best days	1.26%
Minus 30 best days	–1.48%
Minus 40 best days	–3.89%
Minus 50 best days	–6.06%
Minus 60 best days	–8.09%
Minus 70 best days	–9.97%

Source: S&P 500 Accumulation Index.
Period studied: June 1992–June 2002.

have been smart about your choices and invested in solid companies with good earning power or a reputable managed fund with a sound track record, you should sit tight. As the saying goes: the markets have a way of moving money from the impatient to the patient.

Most people, when asked, will say they are in it for the long haul, but volatile markets can put even the toughest of personalities to the test. Pulling out your money when the market is sliding downwards will result in a loss. Hanging in there and waiting for the inevitable turnaround will protect your portfolio and hopefully make you even richer.

6 Higher returns mean higher risk

Different couples can tolerate different amounts of risk. It goes back to your financial personalities and what you are comfortable with. Just as taking high risks is considered unacceptable by many, avoiding risk is also not a particularly good strategy. If you want your money to grow, then some degree of risk is necessary, although you should both be able to sleep at night. High levels of risk in a portfolio mean you could get lucky and make a killing. Equally, you could lose the lot.

Investing in the higher risk asset class of emerging markets may appeal to you, or you may be tempted by a hot share

Figure 9.2 Australian market recovery after crisis: cumulative return of the All Ordinaries

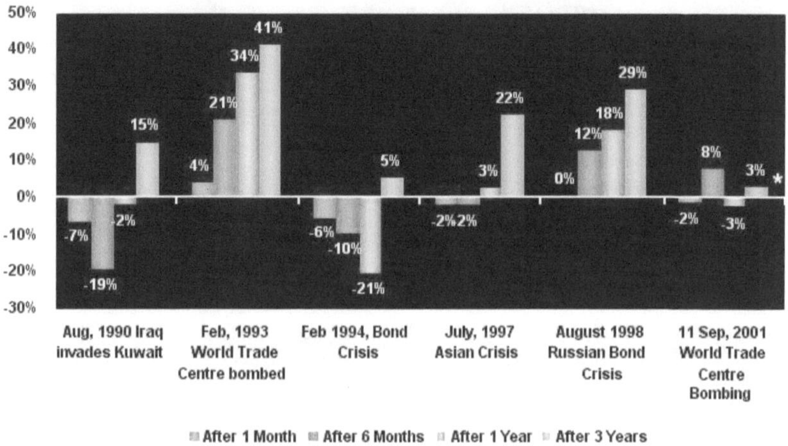

Source: BT, *Datastream*, data at 31 October 2003.

tip. Whatever the investment, if it's high risk you need to be prepared to lose everything. Some couples find that investing in high-risk investments is exciting, but still don't want to risk losing their entire portfolio. In this instance, it may pay to put just a small amount into something racy to see how you go.

Your appetite for risk will also depend on your age. Typically, if you are in your thirties and prepared to invest for the long term, it can pay off. If you are a little older or nearing retirement, you may not feel that there is enough time to recoup any losses. Whatever your decision, you both need to feel comfortable. Otherwise, there may be lingering resentment if you talk your partner into a high-risk venture that doesn't pay off.

7 Invest for growth

For many couples with money to invest, going for growth is the smartest strategy. Growth assets such as shares and property can provide good long-term rewards, particularly if you invest in a reputable managed fund where the selection of stocks has already been made for you. As you also have time on your side, you can afford to take the long-term view necessary when markets experience volatility.

Growth assets also receive quite favourable tax treatment. For example, with assets bought on or after 21 September 1999, only 50 per cent of the capital gain is assessable where the asset is held for more than twelve months.

Investing for growth will also assist you to keep pace with inflation. The benefits of investing in cash can be eroded by inflation over time, however.

Another trap that many couples fall into is investing all of their superannuation in conservative assets. If you are in your twenties, thirties or even forties, consider placing a large proportion of your investment funds—say, 70 per cent—in growth assets as you won't touch these funds for another twenty years or so. As you near retirement, this mix can be closer to 50 per cent growth and 50 per cent fixed interest to accommodate changing needs. Investing for growth early, gives your savings the best opportunity to grow with more time to recoup any potential losses.

8 The need to diversify

You can save all the worry and heartache of rash decisions when markets become volatile by ensuring your portfolio is properly diversified. This means that, as well as property (your own home or a property trust), you should invest in shares—local and international—and fixed interest such as bonds or cash. In this way, should any one of these markets suffer, you haven't risked all your portfolio in the one sector.

Table 9.2 shows the volatility inherent in each sector, and, more specifically, the fact that fortunes fluctuate and it is difficult to predict which sector will outperform.

As you can see, each of the categories has a turn at being the best performer over any given year, which makes it increasingly difficult for investors to know which sector will give them the best return over time. By having a balanced, well-diversified portfolio over all categories, your investments will benefit from

Table 9.2 One year market returns to 30 June (%)

	Australian shares	International shares	Listed property	Australian bonds	International bonds	Cash
2002	–4.5	–23.0	15.5	6.2	3.1	4.6
2001	9.1	–5.7	14.2	7.4	14.5	6.0
2000	15.1	24.2	12.1	6.2	13.7	5.3
1999	15.3	8.6	4.3	3.3	–2.6	5.0
1998	1.6	42.7	10.0	10.9	26.2	5.2
1997	26.6	29.1	28.5	16.8	9.1	6.6
1996	15.8	7.2	3.6	9.4	–9.6	7.8
1995	5.7	14.7	7.9	11.9	22.4	6.8
1994	18.5	0.9	9.8	–1.1	–4.0	4.9
1993	9.9	32.0	17.1	13.9	24.3	5.8

Source: Datastream. S&P/ASX 300 Accumulation Index, MSCI World (ex Aust) Accumulation Index, ASX Listed Property Trusts Index, UBS Warburg Australian Fixed Interest Index, SSB International Bond Index, Liquids Index (BT Funds Management).

upswings in markets as well as being partially cushioned from non-performing asset classes.

The amount that you invest in each of these categories will depend on your age, risk tolerance and income requirements. If you have a well-diversified portfolio, you shouldn't need to make too many changes when markets misbehave—in fact, it may be a good time to increase your holdings in these markets!

9 Dollar-cost averaging

The method of saving known as dollar-cost averaging is a powerful tool. You simply invest a set amount on a regular basis—normally monthly—then take advantage of market fluctuations.

The way it works is that the same amount of units is bought automatically for you (normally in a managed fund) on the

Table 9.3 Dollar-cost averaging

Month	Investment	Unit price	Units purchased
1	$100	$10	10.0
2	$100	$ 8	12.5
3	$100	$ 5	20.0
4	$100	$ 8	12.5
5	$100	$10	10.0
Total	$500		65.0

same day every month. As you would expect, the unit price you buy in at fluctuates with market movements. This means that in some months the unit price you pay will be higher than in others.

For example, say you put $100 a month into a managed investment with an initial unit price of $10. In the next few months, the market falls (causing the unit price to drop) before recovering to its original value (see Table 9.3).

At the end of the five months, you will have 65 units each worth $10, so you have $650. You have invested $500, so your profit is $150 even though the unit price is the same as when you first invested.

Of course, dollar-cost averaging does not guarantee a profit. But with a sensible, long-term approach, it can smooth out the market's ups and downs and reduce the risk of investing in volatile markets.

10 Seek financial advice

As I mentioned in Chapter 3, it is a good idea to seek professional help when deciding on your life investment plan.

You may have done your homework and already decided where you would like your money to go. Even so, it is worthwhile seeking the advice of a professional financial adviser who deals in the financial markets.

10

All about shares

Myth: Investing in shares is too hard for us.
Fact: Sure, it's not for every couple. But if you are interested in the markets and are prepared to do quality research, it can be a rewarding experience.

For couples with little experience, buying and holding shares directly rather than investing in managed funds can be a risky business. If there were a formula for picking the right time to buy shares for maximum growth then we would all be filthy rich! Unfortunately, not even the luckiest couples in the world, clairvoyants or the experts buy at the right time every time. Some say you should only buy at the bottom and sell at the top. That's all very well in theory, but how do you know when the top or the bottom has been reached?

The key to success when buying shares is quality research. One choice is to use the research capabilities of a fund manager or a stockbroker. You can also do your own research on a computer thanks to the Internet. The site www.etradeaustralia.com.au is one of many with a research tool available to the public, providing information about shares, including earnings potential and valuations.

Successful investors are generally very disciplined in their approach and diligently re-weight their portfolio from time to time by looking closely at all of their holdings and other opportunities available in the marketplace.

Experts will advise couples against following the herd or a hot tip when you don't have a good understanding of the company and its profit- or loss-making potential. Likewise, many factors can affect the price of shares, including domestic and world events, investment cycles, competitive pressure and quality of management. Remember, markets are generally efficient and hard to beat, so unless you've got the time and 'the edge', you may do better by employing a professional adviser.

HOW MUCH DO WE NEED?

You don't necessarily need to have a large amount these days to invest in shares. In fact, just a few hundred dollars can get you started. However, if using a stockbroker, you will need to consider the cost of brokerage, so it normally pays to start with a little more to make sure you are getting the best brokerage deal.

If you feel a little nervous about taking the plunge, you may find that a good way to test the waters is to create a mock portfolio. Start by both of you picking three stocks each from across the investment spectrum and pretend to invest $10 000 play money in each stock. Monitor their movements for three months to see what happens. This little trial should give you some confidence to invest real money!

CAN WE BUY AND SELL SHARES IN JOINT NAMES?

Yes, you can. But you have to set up a trading account in both names through a stockbroker. The shares you buy must be in these names. Also, if you are going to have any income from the shares directly debited into a bank account, the bank account also has to be in both names.

Any income that the shares generate will have to be declared separately in your tax returns and be split 50/50.

SHOULD WE BUY SHARES IN THE NAME OF THE LOWER EARNER?

It depends on your tax situation. For instance, take Mia and Tony. He is in the top tax bracket while she has given up work to look after their two-year-old son. Her only income is the interest on their joint bank account. As this puts her in the lowest tax bracket, it would make sense to put the shares in her name. This means that the trading and bank account would need to be in her name only.

With shares, the imputation credits are far more valuable to a partner in a lower tax bracket because they have already been taxed at the company's tax rate of 30 per cent. So, if you are taxed at 30 per cent and the imputation credit is taxed at 30 per cent, no tax should be payable. However, if your partner is in the top tax bracket of 48.5 per cent, there will be tax to pay. If one of you pays no tax then the imputation credit is a simple refund on your tax return.

CAN WE TAKE OUT A JOINT LOAN TO BUY SHARES?

Yes you can. This will not suit every couple because it is best to negatively gear in the name of the individual who is in the highest tax bracket. That's because you will get a bigger tax benefit if you are paying 48.5 per cent in the dollar. However, if you are both in the highest tax bracket, you can put the loan in joint names. For more information on borrowing to invest, see Chapter 11.

HOW DO WE SELECT WHICH SHARES TO BUY?

Share investing requires a commitment of time and self-education. It is wise to enrol in a course or to do some reading on investing and stock selection. There are several publications available, including the daily *Australian Financial Review* and monthly magazines such as *Personal Investor* and *Shares*. For $5, you can attend weekly lunchtime lectures at the Australian Stock Exchange (ASX) and learn from industry practitioners about a vast range of investment securities and issues. The ASX also offers courses on pertinent share investing topics designed specifically for non-professional investors and conducts annual investor days in Sydney, Melbourne, Brisbane, Adelaide and Perth. For further information on ASX services, go to www.asx.com.au. If you do not have Internet access, members of the public are welcome to visit ASX Investor

Centres in capital cities or you can call the ASX information line from anywhere in Australia on 1300 300 279.

Brokers provide clients with research information which is sometimes free and sometimes available for a fee. Research services might include daily market commentaries prior to market opening, global stock market research, and current and archived company research reports. The Securities Institute of Australia conducts courses designed for industry practitioners which are also available to anyone interested in improving their investment knowledge. More detailed course information can be found at www.securities.edu.au.

If all this is too overwhelming, turn on the television. Free-to-air and cable television channels offer a range of programs for non-professional investors.

Remember, for amateur investors it's best to seek the services of a stockbroker or a financial planner. There are simply too many variables and potential pitfalls in doing it yourselves. If you are both savvy types, you can do your company research on the Internet. Read on for more details.

WHEN DO WE BUY AND SELL SHARES?

The best investment advice is simple: buy low and sell high. Since it is impossible to know these two price points without the benefit of hindsight, here are some tips for when to buy and when to sell shares.

When to buy

- *Whenever you can afford to.* Over time, the sharemarket generally outperforms all other types of investment securities, including bonds, cash and property.
- *Broker recommendations.* Sometimes available to clients at no charge, brokerage houses with access to research can provide buy, sell and hold (that is, don't change your shareholding if you already have one) recommendations on some listed companies. If you are unable to do your own research, these types of reports can assist you in your trading decisions.

- If buying stocks for the *long term,* it may be appropriate to buy shares in conservatively managed blue-chip companies with a long, secure track record. Be prepared for some volatility with blue-chip stocks as they are not immune to fluctuations in performance.

When to sell

- *At your stop-loss price.* The best time to sell is when you have achieved your target profit or when the price has lowered to a level at which you are not prepared to take further losses. For more details, see page 136.
- *Key management changes.* The financial performance of a company is in large part due to decisions made by its senior management. When changes in top management occur, this can bring about a fall (or rise) in company share prices.
- *Limited growth prospects coupled with blind diversification.* When a company has exhausted all potential growth opportunities and begins to diversify into businesses with which it has no prior experience, the share price may be compromised. Should the venture prove profitable, the price may rebound. However, the process may take many years.
- *Dissatisfaction with share price performance and company earnings.* Once you have become disenchanted with a company and believe your investment dollars would be more profitable in another stock, it might be wise to cut your losses (or take a profit), sell your stock and move on to another company.

WHAT ARE DISCOUNT BROKERS?

Only a few years ago, a stock broking house offering an online service practically defined it as being a discount broker. Nowadays, just about every large broking house offers an online broking facility at a discount to its full service. Discount brokers execute your buy and sell orders, usually via straight-through processing to the Australian Stock Exchange (ASX). So, if you have done your homework and you know exactly what you want to buy, you have the option of using discount brokers.

However, discount brokers do not provide investment advice or guidance, which is why a full service broker is much more expensive. Some discount broking houses may offer clients research, at a cost in addition to the price of execution.

Some discount brokers

Your Prosperity	www.yourprosperity.com.au	1800 062 061
CommSec	www.commsec.com.au	13 15 19
Netwealth	www.netwealth.com.au	03 9655 1330
Quicken	www.quickBroker.quicken.com.au	1800 720 047
St George Bank	www.quicktrade.com.au	1300 133 500
DSN	www.dsn.com.au	1300 364 134
E-Shares Corporation	www.e-shares.com.au	1300 135 189
Sanford Securities	www.sanford.com.au	1300 360 892

Most discount brokers also offer a telephone service. However, fees are often at a significant premium to Internet-initiated trades. Look out for any special deals your discount broker may run throughout the year.

WHAT IS A BUY-BACK OFFER AND WHEN SHOULD YOU ACCEPT IT?

A buy-back offer occurs when a company has excess capital which it can use either to pay a bigger dividend to its shareholders, buy new businesses, or go to the market and buy back its own shares. This excess capital needs to be used appropriately, otherwise it may affect the performance of the company.

When considering the offer, look at the price and terms of the buy back, compare these with its current share price in the newspaper or through a stockbroker, and speak with a financial planner and/or accountant about the tax implications. If you only have a small holding, it may be a good chance to tidy up your portfolio as the buy back will attract no brokerage fee.

SOME SUPER SHARE TIPS

Thanks to the recent floats in Australia of companies such as the Commonwealth Bank, NRMA (now IAG), Telstra and AMP, millions of people have become investors in the sharemarket. These floats made it as simple as signing on the bottom line and returning a form with a cheque in a self-addressed envelope. As well as being great for the economy, it has given more people a taste of what it is like to own shares in a company.

A friend of mine, Philippa, trades shares from home. Because she understands the markets, many couples ask her how they can buy or sell shares. Here are some of her tips.

- *Only buy shares with money you've set aside for the purpose.* Don't buy shares with money put aside for a deposit on a house, ongoing mortgage payments or next year's school fees.
- *Set a stop-loss position and a realistic profit objective.* Decide on the price at which you will sell your shares if the price falls below your buy price and also the price at which you are prepared to take a profit. If you bought 1000 Telstra shares on 26 June 2002, the investment outlay, excluding brokerage and stamp duty, would have been $4500. If you decided you weren't prepared to lose more than $150 on the investment value, then you would have sold your shareholding once the price fell 15 cents to $4.35 per share. This is your stop-loss price. If you considered a gross profit of $150 to be a realistic profit objective on the investment value, you would have sold your shareholding on 4 July 2002 when the share price closed at $4.85. Although Telstra's share price continued to rise thereafter, reaching $4.93 on 16 July, you would have already made the profit you set out to achieve. Always remember that you cannot lose money making a profit.
- *Once you have received a holding statement from the share registry confirming stock ownership, establish a facility to sell your shares.* You never know when you may want access to your cash, and a lot of stress can be avoided if you set up a broking account before you actually need to use it. A trading account can be established by either speaking to a financial adviser or

by calling any one of the numerous broking houses in the main cities. Stockbroking firms are displayed in the *Yellow Pages* or a list of broking houses can be found at www.infochoice.com.au. This site compares brokers on the basis of services, prices and those with information on upcoming IPOs (Initial Public Offerings, which are the very first sale of stocks to the public). There are four ways to buy and sell shares: via the Internet; following prompts using a mobile or touch phone; by speaking directly to a broker; or by issuing an instruction to an accountant or financial adviser who will pass on the order to a licensed broker for execution. The Internet is the cheapest and fastest way to buy and sell shares. Internet trading can cost as little as $16.30 for a trade where the investment value is less than $10 000 and, unlike bank accounts, you may not need to pay account-keeping fees. If you don't have Internet access at home, you can use facilities at your local library or at an Internet café. Some brokers require that you deposit an opening balance, ranging from $1000 to $5000, to establish a trading account. Most importantly, in selecting a broker, you need to understand the time delay involved in getting your buy and sell order to the market. Some brokers offer straight-through processing (STP), a direct link to the ASX which allows orders to be lodged within seconds. Orders made to brokers without STP may not reach the market for 30 minutes or even longer.

- *When establishing a broking account, convert your shareholdings from issuer sponsored to broker sponsored.* Unless you have specified broker details on the IPO application form, the share registry will provide you with an issuer-sponsored holding statement. By converting your holdings to broker sponsored, when it comes time to sell your shares you can do so immediately without having to prove share ownership to the broker executing the sell order.
- *When applying for shares in IPOs, be sure to use the same form of your name and address in which the broker account is established, and vice versa.* The Clearing House Electronic Sub-register System (CHESS) recognises only exact matches for names

and addresses. For instance, Ms L. Gough is considered different to Ms Linda Gough even if the address details are identical. If personal details do not match exactly, you may need to establish an entirely new broker account to trade that stockholding or liaise with the share registry and your broker to have your details corrected.

- *Try not to have all your investment capital in one stock.* Ideally, spread it across different industries and types of investment securities. Diversification of investments means you diversify your risk. Let's say you bought 1000 Coles Myer shares on 31 December 2001. Excluding brokerage and stamp duty, this acquisition would have cost $8400. By 29 June 2002, the investment was worth $6630 because the share price fell from a cyclical peak of $8.40 to $6.63. In six months, the value of your investment fell $1770. Now let's say you had diversified your investment capital by spreading the original $8400 evenly across two stocks in different industries on 31 December 2001. Half the capital would have acquired 500 Coles Myer shares for $4200. The remainder could have bought 1140 Qantas shares at $3.68 each. The total portfolio value was $8395.20. We already know Coles Myer stock had fallen to $6.63 a share by 29 June 2002. During the same period, the Qantas share price climbed from $3.68 to $4.60. The investment value of the two-company portfolio became $8559—an increase of $163.80. While the shareholding in Coles Myer shares fell by $885, the value of the Qantas investment increased by $1048.80. By holding stock in one company only, investment performance is solely reliant upon movements and developments in one industry and one company. Spreading your investment capital across companies in different industries helps to smooth vast share price movements. Even greater diversification of risk can be achieved by spreading investments across different types of securities—for example, shares and property.
- *Don't expect immediate and dramatic price rises.* Throughout the late 1990s, a plethora of floats hit world stock exchanges and it was expected that buying shares in an IPO ensured a fast profit for investors. While that may have been true

for many floats during the period, you can't assume a profit will happen every time or even at all. In recent years, many stock prices have immediately fallen below the IPO price on the same day they were listed and have never recovered.

- *Buy what you know.* Following the herd does not necessarily mean investment success. During the technology boom of the late 1990s, stories of skyrocketing stock prices constantly made headlines. The tech crash was even bigger news because of the size of fortunes lost. Thousands of investors bought tech stocks without any knowledge of the business or even whether the company had any business at all. Despite consistent quarterly losses reported year after year, the stock price of Amazon.com continued to soar on the back of market enthusiasm for anything technology-based. No doubt many investors made money trading in and out of the stock and many lost money when they got caught in its eventual and oft-predicted crash. Davnet Pty Ltd, a technology stock trading on the ASX, experienced phenomenal price movements in a relatively short time. In July 1999, Davnet was a little-known tech stock trading at about 30 cents a share. By 30 December the same year, its share price was $2.30. Only three months later, the price soared to $5.90. Almost immediately, it began falling. Twelve months later, on 28 March 2001, Davnet shares closed at 27 cents. A year on 28 March 2002, the share price was just three cents. Economists and professional fund managers with years of market experience have difficulty accurately predicting booms and busts and it is even more difficult for non-professional investors to avoid getting caught in a declining market. If you at least have some understanding of the business in which a listed company operates, you are way ahead of those who merely follow the herd.
- *Aim to get it right some of the time, not every time.* Even investment professionals don't get it right every time. If 60 per cent of your investment decisions are profitable, you will most likely remain in the black.

WHAT IS MARGIN LENDING?

Many couples think nothing of going into debt to buy a house, a car or an investment property. But it's a different story when it comes to borrowing to buy shares or managed funds. The concept known as margin lending can be a tax-effective wealth creation strategy. That's because interest on the loan is tax-deductible if it is used for earning income.

If you receive franked dividends—that is, paid out of taxed company profits—from your shares, there are even further tax benefits. By using your existing managed fund or share portfolio as security for a loan, you can boost your portfolio without having to furnish more cash or deal with the capital gains tax implications of disposing of existing investments.

Of course, like any wealth creation venture, there are associated risks, so make sure you seek sound advice from a financial planner before you decide on this strategy.

WHO SHOULD CONSIDER A MARGIN LOAN?

A margin loan could suit you:

- if you are on a high income;
- if you have sufficient cash flow to meet interest payments;
- if there is a strong potential for solid returns;
- if you can tolerate a degree of debt;
- if you can use your investment portfolio, rather than your home, as security.

You can apply for a margin loan through a bank, some fund managers or a stockbroker. You can usually borrow between 50 and 75 per cent of the value of selected shares in your portfolio, secured against the shares themselves.

WHAT IS A MARGIN CALL?

A margin call occurs when the loan balance (the amount you have borrowed) is greater than your loan limit (the amount you can borrow) by more than a designated buffer. If this happens, you may be required to provide more security or pay back some of the loan. If you can't meet these demands, you may have to sell a parcel of your investments and face the possibility of a loss. To reduce the risk of a margin call:

- Adopt a sensible risk management strategy with the help of a financial adviser.
- Make sure you invest in high-quality shares or managed funds.
- Opt to borrow, say, 10 per cent less than your loan limit. This will make a big difference to your risk of a margin call. If you were to borrow up to 65 per cent of your loan limit, your portfolio would need to drop by 13 per cent for a margin call to take place. However, if you took a more conservative option by borrowing up to 30 per cent of your loan limit, your portfolio would need to plummet by as much as 60 per cent in one day before triggering a margin call.
- Reduce your risk further by diversifying across a range of different asset classes through managed funds. This may also result in improved returns.
- Make regular interest payments to help prevent your loan balance and gearing level from increasing.
- Reinvest your dividends and distributions or credit them to your loan to help offset interest charges or reduce your gearing level. This provides an extra guard against a margin call.
- Monitor your investments and loan carefully to ensure you are achieving your aims and are satisfied that the borrowing level is appropriate not only for you, but for the current and future economic climate.

As you can see, this strategy is not for every couple. You will need a relatively high, secure income and will also need adequate cash reserves to meet potential margin calls. Also, be prepared to accept that losses will be magnified the more you are geared. At the same time, if the markets move in your favour, your gains will be multiplied. But if you are timid when it comes to the stockmarket, you may want to consider other options.

11

Get the max from tax

Myth: We have no control over how much tax we pay.
Fact: Education, advice and planning will put you in the driver's seat.

Let's face it, no one likes paying tax but it's a fact of life. Understanding what tax you should pay and what deductions you can claim can be confusing, as the rules keep changing. Having said that, tax has been around for thousands of years and is here to stay so it's a good idea for couples to take advantage of legitimate means of reducing their tax bills.

A word of warning: be wary of investing in anything with the sole purpose of receiving a tax deduction. Michael Dirkis, tax director at the Taxation Institute of Australia, warns that getting a deduction is always the cream to what should be a good business investment. If it's a property and the rental return and the price is good, that should be why you are buying it. If you get a few gains out of the tax side, it makes it even better. You really don't want to be pouring money down an interest drain to find out that you haven't made a capital gain just for a tax deduction.

If you are chasing something merely for a tax advantage, you have lost the point of why you are investing. If you want to chase long odds then go to the races. You really need to ask the hard questions. Is this a good investment? What am I going to be doing in ten years? How are we going to service the loan? Looking ahead, are we both going to be working? At what point in time are we planning to have children? What if something happens in between? Those steps can all be worked through with a financial planner, but at the same time, make sure you have the tax side covered.

SIX WAYS TO TRIM YOUR TAX

1 Income splitting

You could be forgiven for forgetting to focus on the tax angle when you buy your first home together or make an investment in joint names. After all, it's not something that immediately comes to mind. Once you are a couple, it's all too easy to fall into the trap of believing that all your investments should be in joint names.

But if you take time to plan, there may be significant tax advantages to holding investments in only one name, particularly if one partner is earning much less than the other. Before you embark on any key investment decisions, reaffirm your life goals with your partner. Would you like to have children? If so, when? Is one of you planning to take time off to study at some point? Is there a large discrepancy in your incomes and is this likely to continue? Planning and preparing for changes in income levels are vital if you want to get the max from tax.

In the case of Samantha and Hugh, he was earning $65 000 a year while she worked part-time after leaving a full-time position to raise their young son, Danny. Her income was $16 500. They had $30 000 in savings which they were keen to invest in a managed fund. Neither had considered the merits of having the investment in Samantha's name.

Fortunately, they wanted to make sure they were doing the right thing and made an appointment with a financial planner who came highly recommended. The planner agreed with their decision to invest the money, but suggested that it would be far better to put it in Samantha's name to reduce the tax they would pay on the income from the investment. This is known as income splitting.

The planner also suggested that, rather than putting the

money in just one fund, they would be better to diversify by investing in two different managed funds.

The savings are as follows. Assume the $30 000 investment earns a 5 per cent assessable return—that is, $1500 a year. Samantha would pay tax at 18.5 per cent including Medicare, which means the after-tax return would be $1222.50. If the investment was in Hugh's name, he would pay tax at 48.5 per cent, so his after-tax return would be only $772.50—in other words, they would be $450 out of pocket. (Table 11.1 lists Australian tax rates—to which 1.5 per cent for the Medicare levy needs to be added.)

However, if the couple were planning to use their savings to negatively gear an investment property, then the decision about whose name to invest in would depend on who has the higher income to reap the best tax benefit.

Of course, if you or your partner feels uneasy about having an investment in just one name, put it in both names.

The same principle applies if you're planning on investing for your children's future. Say Samantha and Hugh decided to put the $30 000 investment in their son's name. If income from the investments exceeded the child's tax threshold of $416 a year, Danny, aged five, would be subject to a tax rate of 66 per cent (minus a $150 low-income tax offset) for a gap between $416 and $1445 (as of June 2003). Anything above that is taxed at 48.5 per cent. Remember, it is only worthwhile putting it in the parent's name if their tax rate is below the top marginal rate.

I know 66 per cent sounds like an outrageously high rate, but it's there for a good reason: to claw back the $416 threshold in order to ensure every dollar of unearned income is taxed at the top marginal rate. This type of income is only subject to these rules if the children didn't earn the money themselves—for example, if it was a gift from the parent or grandparent. But if the child has a paper run or worked in a local corner shop and has invested the proceeds in a bank account and it attracts interest over a number of years, that interest is taxed at normal rates. (Visit www.ato.gov.au and follow the prompts for tax information on minors.)

So if you are keen to set up a fund for your children and it is likely to attract the 66 per cent tax rate, put it in the parent's name provided their marginal tax rate is below the top marginal rate. When the children are older—and can afford to pay their own tax bills—you can give them the money (note that there may be transaction costs in relation to this—for example, stamp duty, brokerage or realisation of a capital gain).

Investing in your children's future requires a long-term focus. So aim for investments that offer high growth opportunities. If in doubt, seek advice.

Table 11.1 Australian taxation rates for residents, 2003–2004*

Taxable income	Tax on this income
$0–6000	Nil
$6001–20 000	17c for each $1 over $6000
$20 001–50 000	$2380 plus 30c for each $1 over $20 000
$50 001–60 000	$11 380 plus 42c for each $1 over $50 000
$60 000 plus	$15 580 plus 47c for each $1 over $60 000

* Medicare levy of 1.5 per cent usually applies to income in excess of $14 000. Note that the above rates do not include the Medicare levy.

2 Borrowing to buy

I have talked about this topic before (see Chapters 8 and 10 in particular), but negative gearing is worth mentioning again as it can be an effective tax strategy. Not only can you increase your joint exposure to the property or stock market, you can use someone else's money and gain a tax benefit at the same time. Most running costs associated with the loan used to buy the assets—including interest charges—are deductible if they exceed the income generated by the investments. It is also possible to offset the loss against other income such as salary or wages (although generally not capital gains) and is useful if either of you is in a higher tax bracket.

Having said that, you do need to consider a number of issues.

Negative gearing can be useful when you have a high disposable income and there is also a high capital gain. However, in a slow market—for example, if the property market were to drop and stagnate—then negative gearing doesn't make any sense because you are not getting a capital return. In the long term, provided there is inflation and market increases, negative gearing on property may be a good option. The same goes for negatively gearing into shares—it makes good sense but, as with everything else, make sure you have a balanced portfolio and diversify as much as possible.

So timing is important when it comes to negative gearing. When property markets are booming and interest rates are low, it may not be a sound strategy to negatively gear into property. This is because the cost of your property may be at the top end, leaving little room for growth in the short term. It may also be more difficult to find a tenant to rent your property if everyone else is buying up investment properties at the same time. If, on the other hand, the property market eases and interest rates start to rise slightly, this can be a better time to include a negatively geared property in your portfolio. Of course, you will need to have sufficient income to subsidise any shortfall in interest repayments, particularly if rates are on the rise.

3 Juggle in June

While there is little you can do about interest being paid to you from banks or financial institutions at the end of the financial year, you can reorganise your affairs to minimise the impact. Say you have made a loss on one of your investments and a capital gain on another. To minimise the tax on your capital gain (which is added to your income and taxed at your marginal rate plus the Medicare levy) you can realise—or sell—the investment that has lost money and offset it against your capital gain.

Remember, capital losses can only be offset against capital gains, not against other income. However, if you don't have any capital gains to offset, you can carry forward any losses for future years. Some financial institutions can provide an estimated tax position on their managed funds prior to 30 June. It is worth contacting your funds a few weeks before the end of a financial year so that you can make changes to your investments.

If you are both planning a holiday around tax time and are thinking of asking for holiday pay in advance, you may wish to consider delaying your trip until after the end of the financial year. As salary and wages are taxed when paid, not when they are earned, it will help to smooth out your tax instead of lumping it into the previous year's income.

4 Use an offset account

An offset account attached to your mortgage is another great way to reduce your tax on income earned. Put simply, you have two accounts: a savings account and loan account. With an offset arrangement, the balance of your savings account offsets the amount of your mortgage on which interest is chargeable. The advantage is that you will reduce the size of your mortgage.

Say you have a mortgage of $100 000 with an interest rate of 7 per cent and an offset (savings) account with a balance of $5000. In a normal savings account, you will be taxed on any interest earned on your $5000. With an offset account, you will pay interest of 7 per cent only on $95 000 instead of the full amount. This, in effect, will reduce the interest payable on your loan and the term of the loan itself.

5 Franked dividends

In 1987, the government introduced dividend imputation (often referred to as franking credits) to encourage Australians to save. So if a company you have invested in—either through a direct share holding or managed fund—has already paid tax at the full corporate rate of 30 per cent, you will receive a tax credit for the tax paid by the company on income passed down to you in the form of a distribution.

Some companies don't pay the full tax rate, in which case you will receive only partly franked dividends. This tax break only relates to Australian companies.

There are also products on the market that are labelled 'imputation funds'. One of their aims is to invest in companies that pay franked or partially franked dividends. As I've mentioned, it is important to focus on the overall performance of a fund or company rather than relying on any tax break. But if you find an investment with good earnings potential that pays some franking credits, you will be ahead of the game.

6 Salary packaging

By taking advantage of salary packaging, you can make better use of the money you earn before actually being paid. Depending on where you work, you may be able to fund car finance, tools of the trade (laptops, mobile phones, etc.), child care and superannuation payments in pre-tax dollars.

But how do you find out what your employer can provide and how do you find out about the implications of Fringe Benefits Tax (FBT)? Simply make a few calls to your pay office or human resources department to find out whether they offer salary packaging; you may be able to make some smart savings and they should also be able to tell you what the tax treatment will be.

It's often timely to negotiate salary packaging deals when starting a new job or at the beginning of the financial year. And don't think this applies only to high-flying executives. Depending on the flexibility of your employer, there are no real restrictions on who can offer salary packaging.

One of the best ways is contributing to superannuation from your pre-tax salary over and above what your employer pays on your behalf. This is called salary sacrificing into super and is discussed in more detail in Chapter 12. Another way to take advantage of your 'joint' status is to contribute super for your spouse or de facto as long as you are not permanently separated and your partner is aged under 65. This works well if your partner is employed part-time or is at home looking after the family. The tax advantages are that you can claim an 18 per cent rebate on the spouse contributions you make each year. If your partner earns $10 800 or less, you can claim the rebate on up to $3000 of spouse contributions with the maximum rebate being $540. Each dollar that your partner earns over this amount reduces the amount by one dollar of the contribution you can claim a rebate on. There is no rebate if your spouse's assessable income is higher than $13800.

Aside from superannuation, many employers offer salary packaging for car finance, financial planning, income protection insurance, work-related training courses and tools of the trade. Again, you can use salary sacrificing to make tax savings. Effectively, you can give yourself a pay rise by simply making better use of an existing salary package. If a company has a child care centre, you can pay for that in pre-tax dollars too. The same goes for certain on-site parking, taxi travel to and from work and relocation costs such as air fares and removal fees if moving interstate.

For employees, there are several advantages. Not only do you make tax savings but you benefit from increased flexibility by structuring your remuneration to suit your needs at different stages in your life. For example, paying off a car in a cost-effective way may be more attractive earlier in your career, while amassing superannuation may be more appealing later on.

SEEK HELP

Always seek out a helping hand. You cannot possibly be expected to know all the new tax rulings or understand the intricacies of tax legislation, nor can you rely on friends or colleagues to help you keep on top. There are many ways you can educate yourselves, particularly if you have access to the Internet.

Websites such as that of the Australian Taxation Office at www.ato.gov.com.au have a tax planning section which will take you to the Tax Planning Professionals site. This site can help with tax-effective investments, superannuation and managed investments, as well as other advice. It can also help you to complete your tax return online and provides a year-round service to answer any of your tax questions.

If you are starting a small business and want to know what tax you will need to pay, visit www.business.gov.au/BEP2002/Syndication/ChannelList/.

If your questions relate to family allowances or tax benefits, try the Family Assistance Office at www.familyassist.gov.au, or phone 13 61 50.

USE AN ACCOUNTANT

For many couples, it's also a good idea to have an accountant—along with an accredited financial planner—as part of your finance team, as they can help to streamline your affairs and make the most of the tax system.

You can keep your accountant's bill down by being organised and not turning up to your first appointment with a shoebox bulging with receipts. You can't beat a lever arch file with an alphabetic divider as a means of keeping your affairs in order. As a dividend or bank statement comes in, you simply file it away. This will take much of the pain out of preparing for tax time. To further keep costs down, reduce the time spent on the phone to your accountant and ask about the most efficient way to present your tax details.

Expect to pay anywhere from $100 to more than $300 an hour for an accountant's services, depending on where they work and the position they hold. Partners in big accounting firms, for example, will charge the top rate.

In gathering your details, don't forget your tax offsets, including your health insurance rebate. If you have misplaced this information, contact your insurer. You should also find out about any medical expenses rebate, details of which can be obtained from Medicare. If you have spent more than $1500 (in the 2003–04 financial year) on medical expenses after any reimbursements from your health fund or Medicare, you can claim in excess of 20 cents in the dollar.

If you decide to prepare your own tax returns, make sure you declare all your income, attach all your group certificates and claim the correct deductions. Don't forget to include any income from bank accounts that you may have closed during the year. And, to avoid penalties, file your return by the required date (usually 31 October).

LODGING YOUR RETURN

There are a number of different ways to lodge tax returns. Whether you do it electronically, by hand or with the help of a tax agent or accountant will depend on your own ability, time constraints, your job and the complexities of your investments.

If you are average wage earners, it may be easier—and cheaper—to use the Australian Taxation Office's free electronic *Tax Pack* (e-tax) which should deliver any refunds in fourteen days. Refunds based on paper returns can take up to six weeks to arrive.

With e-tax, you can also obtain an estimate of your tax refund. The software package, used by more than 280 000 people in 2001, relies on the highest levels of security technology. Access e-tax by following the prompts from www.ato.gov.au. If you do not make use of a tax agent, you will need to lodge your return by 31 October each year to avoid penalties. Tax agents can request extensions of this date.

If you do not have to lodge a return but wish to claim the new baby bonus—a payment for Australian families who have had a baby or gained legal responsibility for a child after 30 June 2001—you can also use e-tax.

If you prefer to hand over responsibility for your tax returns to a professional, you can choose a basic tax agent or an accountant. Both can lodge your returns electronically and their fees are tax deductible.

If you have an investment property, share portfolio or complicated deductions, it may be better to use an accountant who should be up to date with developments on the tax landscape. Sure, it will cost you more in fees but you should save in the long term by claiming the right deductions and avoiding hefty penalties for underpaying tax.

SALARY SACRIFICING FOR SAME-SEX COUPLES

Salary sacrificing can be used as an effective planning tool for same-sex couples. That's because, as the *Fringe Benefits Tax Act* currently stands, it does not apply to same-sex couples. However, such payments will usually be assessable for tax purposes to the recipient.

This means that same-sex couples can salary sacrifice to great effect. The employer of the higher income partner can, for example, make mortgage payments to the other same-sex partner or provide car benefits and not be subject to FBT. At present, any such arrangements must be negotiated at the start of your contract with your employer and must be for a specific purpose—that is, a goodwill gesture in paying the mortgage of a same-sex partner on a property owned by that person (not the person making the salary sacrifice).

END-OF-YEAR TAX SCHEMES

Many people will have heard of fantastic end-of-year schemes that promise to save thousands in tax. If so, proceed with caution. You need to do your homework. For sophisticated investors, it's a matter of judgment. For unsophisticated investors, you want to make sure you have a product ruling indicating that the scheme is legitimate. But this will not guarantee its commercial success. Says Michael Dirkis:

> You really want to make sure that the product you are buying is not an end-of-year scheme just to get rid of money to avoid tax. You want to ensure all the fundamentals under those arrangements are going to come to fruition. If you are going to invest in olives, tomatoes or alpacas, are you going to get returns going forward? What is the market history of that product?
>
> The problem with most of these new areas is that there is no history of returns and so it tends to be speculative. It's a bit like investing in movies. About 90 per cent of movies fail so not everyone is going to get the sort of returns investors got when they put their money into *Crocodile Dundee*.

The ATO has put together a Website which provides a checklist for investors to help sort out what is legitimate. See www.ato.gov.au/atp. If you are still determined to proceed, get independent professional advice from an accountant or financial planner.

FAMILY TAX BENEFITS

Raising a family is hard work and financially draining, so it is important to know what you are entitled to claim from the government and how to go about getting it. In Australia since 1 July 2000, there have been three easy-to-understand payments that can be claimed to assist families in raising their children.

1 *Family Tax Benefit Part A.* This helps with the cost of raising children. To receive the Part A benefit, your joint income will be assessed. These payments are most beneficial to families with a combined income of less than $29 857 a year and scale down for income earned over that threshold. If you are eligible for this benefit, you will also be eligible for a one off maternity allowance payment.
2 *Family Tax Benefit Part B.* Provides extra help for families with one income, including sole parents. To receive this payment, no income is taken into account for sole parents. Sole parents receive the maximum rate of benefits, irrespective of income. This amount is paid in addition to the Family Tax Benefit Part A.
3 *Child care benefit.* Helps with the cost of child care. Your combined income is taken into account but higher income families are still eligible for some payments. There are two types of care: registered and approved. The former is when you pay a nanny, friends, relatives or care services outside school hours. Approved care includes family day-care centres, at-home care, before- and after-school care and some occasional care.

Visit the Website www.familyassist.gov.au or phone 13 61 50 to find out more, or where your nearest Family Assistance office is located.

BABY BONUS

At the time of writing, the baby bonus was granted to women who either gave birth or adopted a child after 30 June 2001.

To assist in calculating the baby bonus, which is based on your income, visit the ATO Website at www.ato.gov.com.au. To claim the bonus, you should complete and lodge a claim form via e-tax on the Internet when you lodge your tax return, or see an accountant or tax agent.

THE CLAIM GAME

For many people, working from home as a contractor offers the advantage of flexibility and a chance to continue a career that may have stalled or been sidelined to raise a family. There are many other positives—for instance, you can swap your corporate clobber for the more comfy uniform of shorts and a t-shirt! But there are several disadvantages, largely to do with money.

As a business operator, when your computer suffers a file-threatening virus, it's you who has to organise—and pay—to have it removed. When you run out of fax/printer paper, it's you who has to pay for the next batch. And when the courier comes to collect a package, it's you who has to fork out for the service.

However, such expenses may be deductible if you satisfy certain requirements under what's called the alienation of personal services provisions. For example, if at least 75 per cent of your income is derived from services where you are paid to achieve a specific result, you provide all the tools you need and face commercial risk, including liability for defective work, such deductions may be available. This test is known as the 'results test'.

However, where the above test is not satisfied and 80 per cent or more of your income is derived from one client, you will need to apply for a determination from the tax office to claim such deductions.

Where the results test is not satisfied and 80 per cent or more of your income is *not* derived from one client, other criteria must be satisfied before certain deductions are available. If in doubt, check with a tax agent.

The home office

There are many deductions you can claim to reduce your tax bill and boost your net income. For example, if you work from home, you may be able to claim the additional costs of carrying out that work—for example, a portion of your power bill arising from extra lighting, cooling or heating; insurance costs for office equipment; and depreciation of curtains, blinds, carpets, rugs, desk, desk chair, filing cabinet, computer, telephone, fax, computer, printer, scanner, and so on. You usually have to write them off over their effective life—four years for a desk computer and eight years for most office furniture.

Depending on the structure of your business, if your home is your principal place of business and you do not have another office or desk elsewhere, you may be entitled to claim what's known as the holding costs, which is a portion of your rent or mortgage in respect of the percentage of the area you use as an office. For example, if your office is 30 per cent of your total house space, you may deduct 30 per cent of your rent or mortgage interest. But the ATO insists that this area must be for exclusive use and be distinguishable from the rest of your home.

There is also the risk that you may be liable for capital gains tax if and when you sell your property. Your principal place of residence is normally free of capital gains tax so check with your accountant first.

You may also claim other expenses such as business phone calls, Internet use, phone rental, connection costs for a second designated line (which will eliminate any doubts over work-related calls), stationery, books, repairs, accountancy and book-keeping fees.

Sadly, claiming for a babysitter or child care does not qualify under the legislation as it is private in nature.

When paying for your expenses as a business operator, it may be easier to use a credit card rather than having to rely on lots of receipts to support your claims. But keep in mind that many businesses offer better deals for cash over credit.

Before deciding on how to set up your business, consult an accountant. Keep accurate records and consider employing a book-keeper to ease the pain of meeting your taxation commitments and keeping arguments to a minimum!

Car costs

Any car costs—such as maintenance, a proportion of your petrol bill, etc.—may also be claimed, provided you maintain the required documentation. There are four methods to calculate the amount of deductible car expenses:

1. cents per kilometre method (only applicable if travel is less than 5000 kilometres);
2. 12 per cent of original value method (only applicable if travel is more than 5000 kilometres);
3. one-third of actual expenses method (only applicable if travel is more than 5000 kilometres and expenses must be appropriately substantiated);
4. log book method.

The log book method is the most common and you will need to establish the percentage of time you use your car for work. If it's used for, say, 50 per cent, keep travel details to support your claim. A vehicle log book, bought from newsagents, is the best way to keep track of the distance travelled.

As well, you may prefer to lease or buy a car on hire purchase and claim depreciation (up to the luxury depreciation limit) and a portion of the interest payments.

CAPITAL GAINS TAX

Some say that capital gains tax (CGT) was invented only to stop the rich getting richer. That may be so, but it seems that it touches all of us at some point in our lives. However, unlike income tax which we pay annually, CGT is generally only paid when we sell an asset. So whether it's shares or an investment property, we are forced to think about the potential tax liability before we make any decisions.

From 21 September 1999, the government introduced a new method of calculating CGT for individuals. Under the old regime, where shares were held for longer than twelve months, CGT was paid on the difference between the sale proceeds and the indexed cost base (the cost base of the asset indexed to movements in the consumer price index during the period the asset was held). Where the investment was held for less than twelve months, the cost base was not indexed.

Now, individual investors have a choice between the indexed cost base method (this is now frozen at the September 1999 rate) or a 50 per cent discount on CGT where an asset is held for more than twelve months. Basically, this means that, of the gain made on any investment held for over twelve months, only 50 per cent is assessable for tax purposes. Note that the 50 per cent discount applies to the capital gain after the application of any capital losses. Remember, as we mentioned earlier, you can reduce your CGT bill even further by offsetting any capital gains against capital losses.

Say you both invested in a technology stock and lost $1000. On the other hand, you did well on some Australian shares and managed to turn a $2000 investment into $3000. Thus you can offset the gain of $1000 against your loss of $1000 and pay no CGT. A much better scenario!

Assets bought before the introduction of CGT in September 1985 are exempt. Also, your family home is exempt unless you have rented it out and declared the income, along with any relevant tax deductions. However, you can rent it out for up to six years and not lose the exemption.

FAMILY TRUSTS

If you're a family with substantial assets or there is an individual in the family in a position where there are professional and public liability risks, then a family trust may be a suitable investment vehicle. The key advantages of trusts are asset protection (from bankruptcy and relationship breakdown), CGT discount and estate planning (see Chapter 14). The negative is you have to distribute every cent you earn every year.

They also offer flexibility in distributing capital and dealing with income, particularly if the beneficiaries attract low personal tax rates—for example, a university student. Also, if your partner is retrenched and you have a family trust, he or she can receive an income distribution. Seek legal advice on the conditions applying to trust distributions.

12

Take the super highway

Myth: We're not old enough to worry about superannuation.
Fact: If you act now, you'll be better placed for the retirement you want rather than the retirement you get stuck with.

Whenever superannuation is mentioned, most couples' eyes start to glaze over. It's hard to imagine life in retirement when you are still working your way up the corporate ladder or raising a family—it all seems so far away.

It doesn't help that, at first glance, superannuation seems so difficult to understand. Many of us also believe that our employer will have it all under control. In fact, ING's research has found that more than 60 per cent of respondents do not even know the name of their super fund. Many don't know how much they have invested, where it is invested and what fees they are being charged. Yet if you asked the same questions about their share portfolio, their responses would be surprisingly different.

So why all the hype? As I have already mentioned, Australians have one of the worst saving rates in the world, tucking away just 4 per cent of their income, according to the Australian Bureau of Statistics. This fact alone poses a big problem for the government, not to mention our ageing population or the baby-boomer generation who represent a big slice of the population. This group will start to retire in the next five or so years and will make a big dent in the government's coffers. As a result, it will become increasingly difficult to meet everyone's needs and there is a strong possibility that the age pension will be much harder to access. By investing enough money in super, you will be taking control of your future without having to rely solely on the age pension.

Like most couples, your financial goals may be focused on the short or medium term and geared towards a desirable lifestyle now rather than in the future. However, this is short-sighted and may prove costly. Thanks to medical advances, Australians may spend over 30 years in retirement, which is almost as long as they will spend in the workforce. That's a scary thought if your superannuation investments provide you as a couple with a somewhat paltry $20 000 a year to live on. Retiring on such an income will force many couples to downgrade their lifestyles.

WHAT'S SO GREAT ABOUT SUPER?

Superannuation is one of life's legitimate tax breaks. It is still one of the best vehicles for people to grow their investments at the same time as offering worthwhile tax savings.

Your investments in super will also provide you with financial independence and security to enjoy a comfortable lifestyle in retirement, assuming that you have accumulated enough. To illustrate this point, a survey of retirees by peak superannuation body the Association of Superannuation Funds of Australia (ASFA), titled *Looking Forward to Retirement . . . Is This as Good as it Gets?* has found that retirement can be a daily compromise where individuals keep a close eye on spending while presiding over a 'shrinking horizon of reduced opportunities'. However, for those on higher retirement incomes, the research has revealed that it can also be a period of liberation and expanding horizons as retirees are freed of the ties of work and are able to meet their post-career expectations. The report says:

> In this regard, it is superannuation and other private retirement savings which does the liberating. The age pension prevents poverty, but even its strongest supporters would struggle to claim it is liberating.

Provided you invest further funds to top up the contributions your employer makes on your behalf, your super will probably be the biggest asset you both own—bigger even than your family home. It could be the difference between a struggle to make ends meet and one of the most stress-free and enjoyable periods of your lives together.

You may also be able to take out extra life insurance cover through your super fund. Many have some degree of automatic life cover, while others offer a choice of life, disability and salary continuance cover.

In reality, superannuation is just as important as your other investments—indeed, some would argue it is more important—and should be given as much attention. It is invested in the same countries and asset classes as your other savings; the biggest difference is in the tax treatment.

HOW MUCH SUPER DO WE NEED?

Not only do many couples neglect to focus on saving for their retirement, they also have unrealistic expectations of what they think they will need. According to the ASFA research, the target for a minimum retirement income for a person on average weekly earnings should initially be set at \$25 000 a year in today's dollars, rising to \$30 000 for those retiring in 2030. However, most participants surveyed were seeking a retirement income in excess of \$30 000 each and many were looking for more than \$40 000 a year. Even low-income earners were hoping for something better when they retired. The problem is that our expectations may often exceed the end balance in our super account.

Experts tend to be divided on how much you will need to save but the general consensus is that you should aim for 75 per cent of your final salary. For example, if your final salary is \$50 000 a year then you should aim for \$37 500 a year in retirement. Of course, you will need to factor in your goals for retirement and the lifestyle you desire.

Employers must make Superannuation Guarantee (SG) contributions of 9 per cent of your salary to super. On this basis, to reach your retirement income goals you may need to contribute at least 7–8 per cent more, bringing your total super contribution to 16 per cent.

The longer you delay investing additional amounts into super, the less you will have on retirement. By starting earlier, you will also relieve the pressure later in life, when school fees and mortgage payments eat into more of your salary. Don't despair if you are already in your thirties or forties. It's not too late, but you will need to contribute even more to catch up.

Of course, how much super you both need will depend on a number of factors, including your desired lifestyle, when you retire and what other income or assets you have. Table 12.1 provides a guide to how much you will need to contribute to achieve the income you are looking for in retirement.

A TALE OF TWO INCOMES

Naomi and Jack were pretty relaxed about super. After all, the government was supposed to have it all under control—that's why it kept increasing the employer contributions each year so that the average person in the street didn't have to worry.

Jack was in and out of work but hoped to be employed until retirement age. Naomi had not returned to work since having their second child. When questioned about how much they thought they would need, they calculated that their outgoings would be significantly less since they wouldn't have a mortgage. A combined income of $20 000 a year should do it, or so they thought.

Susan and Joe, on the other hand, increased their contributions when they were in their thirties. Consequently, their nest egg would eventually reward them with a combined income of more than $40 000 a year.

Based on ASFA research, here's what the two couples could afford with their super.

Naomi and Jack: $20 000 combined annual income

Food: Limited meat and fruit and vegetables with no trimmings.
Electricity: Only a one-bar radiator and limited hot showers.

Clothing: Rarely able to buy new clothes except to replace worn ones.
Entertainment: Low-cost meals at a local club, holidays at home.
Transport: A struggle to maintain one car.
Personal care: Two haircuts a year each. Forget beauty treatments, massages or yoga classes!

Susan and Joe: $40 000-plus combined annual income

Food: Good quality cuts of meat, seafood and other deli items.
Electricity: Central heating/air conditioner for limited periods.
Clothing: Several new outfits and pairs of shoes each.
Entertainment: Regular trips to the theatre, able to dine out at moderate restaurants, buy some books and go interstate for a holiday.
Transport: Able to keep and maintain one car.
Personal care: Regular visits to a hairdresser, beautician, massage therapist and yoga classes.

If you expect more from your retirement, it is essential to do your sums. What you might think is enough to retire on may not in fact be the case. By starting now and using some simple strategies, such as salary sacrificing and choosing growth assets instead of cash, you will be well on the way to achieving the future lifestyle you want.

YOUR SUPER CHOICES

Industry funds

Historically, industry funds were designed to service employees from the blue-collar sector who typically belonged to a union. These days, industry funds are increasingly opening their doors to direct investors by gaining public-offer status. Their main attraction is low administrative fees.

Master funds

Increasingly popular, master funds combine a choice of investments and provide consolidated reporting on super. You can

Table 12.1 Yearly saving required to fund retirement at age 65

Income required on retirement (on today's $)									
	30,000	40,000	50,000	60,000		30,000	40,000	50,000	60,000
	Annual contribution required ($)					Annual contribution required ($)			
	Male 25-year-old					Female 25-year-old			
0	6,192	8,257	10,321	12,385	**0**	7,391	9,855	12,319	14,782
5,000	5,923	7,987	10,051	12,115	**5,000**	7,121	9,585	12,049	14,512
10,000	5,653	7,717	9,781	11,845	**10,000**	6,851	9,315	11,779	14,243
20,000	5,113	7,177	9,241	11,306	**20,000**	6,312	8,775	11,239	13,703
30,000	4,573	6,638	8,702	10,766	**30,000**	5,772	8,236	10,700	13,163
40,000	4,034	6,098	8,162	10,226	**40,000**	5,232	7,696	10,160	12,624
50,000	3,494	5,558	7,622	9,687	**50,000**	4,693	7,156	9,620	12,084
	Male 30-year-old					Female 30-year-old			
0	7,826	10,434	13,043	15,651	**0**	9,340	12,454	15,567	18,681
5,000	7,537	10,146	12,754	15,363	**5,000**	9,052	12,165	15,279	18,392
10,000	7,249	9,857	12,466	15,074	**10,000**	8,763	11,877	14,990	18,104
20,000	6,672	9,280	11,880	14,497	**20,000**	8,186	11,300	14,413	17,527
30,000	6,094	8,703	11,312	13,920	**30,000**	7,609	10,723	13,836	16,950
40,000	5,517	8,126	10,734	13,343	**40,000**	7,032	10,146	13,259	16,373
50,000	4,940	7,549	10,157	12,766	**50,000**	6,455	9,569	12,682	15,796
	Male 35-year-old					Female 35-year-old			
0	10,074	13,432	16,790	20,147	**0**	12,024	16,032	20,039	24,047
5,000	9,759	13,117	16,475	19,833	**5,000**	11,709	15,717	19,725	23,733
10,000	9,445	12,803	16,161	19,519	**10,000**	11,395	15,403	19,411	23,419
20,000	8,817	12,175	15,532	18,890	**20,000**	10,767	14,774	18,782	22,790
30,000	8,188	11,546	14,904	18,262	**30,000**	10,138	14,146	18,154	22,162
40,000	7,560	10,917	14,275	17,633	**40,000**	9,509	13,517	17,525	21,533
50,000	6,931	10,289	13,647	17,005	**50,000**	8,881	12,889	16,897	20,905
	Male 40-year-old					Female 40-year-old			
0	13,309	17,745	22,181	26,617	**0**	15,885	21,180	26,475	31,769
5,000	12,957	17,393	21,830	26,266	**5,000**	15,533	20,828	26,123	31,418
10,000	12,606	17,042	21,478	25,915	**10,000**	15,182	20,477	25,772	31,067
20,000	11,903	16,340	20,776	25,212	**20,000**	14,479	19,774	25,069	30,364
30,000	11,201	15,637	20,073	24,509	**30,000**	13,777	19,072	24,367	29,662
40,000	10,498	14,934	19,370	23,807	**40,000**	13,074	18,369	23,664	28,959
50,000	9,795	14,232	18,668	23,104	**50,000**	12,372	17,667	22,961	28,256

Source: BT *Superbook*

Assumptions: 6.5% net return in super fund. Retirement income based on payment of benefit as a lifetime pension, single life, 4.5% net return, indexed at 3%. Annual contribution to super based on regular monthly contribution. Surcharge is assured to be nil. Contributions tax at 15%. No entry fees assured. A small change in one of the assumptions may result in a large change in the final result.

switch between fund managers and different types of asset classes relatively easily, often without the need to fill in application forms as the service is online. Financial advisers find this product useful in tailoring individual portfolios for clients according to their risk profile and retirement goals.

For couples, an added bonus of some master funds, and increasingly industry funds and some larger corporate funds, is the ability to set up an account for your spouse whether or not they are working. This is particularly useful if you are a member of a master fund through your employer and your spouse is self-employed and able to choose any super fund for their contributions. In this instance, your spouse is able to set up their own account and have access to a range of investments, insurance and the lower fees available to investors of a master fund. To find out if your employer offers this facility, contact your human resources department.

Personal super plans

Personal super plans tend to suit small to medium companies and self-employed people and are usually offered by financial institutions such as insurance companies. They are a type of managed fund and have two key advantages: portability and flexibility. If you leave your job, you do not have to worry about transferring your super.

You also have some say about where your money goes, which can give you a sense of control, security and independence. However, they may be more expensive than employer or industry funds so check entry, exit and annual management fees.

Company funds

Usually offered by large businesses, these are created by an employer for the benefit of company employees. They are sometimes called an employer-sponsored fund. Investors in these funds may need to roll over their account balance to another fund if they leave their job and they may or may not be offered a choice of investment.

Do-it-yourself

For those couples who want to consolidate their funds, who wish to have more control of their investments, and who have the necessary money, time and interest, a self-managed superannuation fund may be worth considering. They are fast becoming popular, particularly with small-business owners and the self-employed, with recent figures showing there are more than 240 000 self-managed funds in Australia. But be aware that the ideal trustee of such a fund is a lover of spreadsheets, investments and paperwork.

Of course, having two people investing under the one umbrella will give you greater access to wholesale rates and returns.

Opinion varies on the minimum balance recommended to set up a self-managed fund, but it ranges from $100 000 to $300 000. However, the final decision about whether it is worthwhile for you will depend upon how the costs compare with the alternatives. The fund should only be created if you are keen to put in the time and effort to set it up properly, then closely monitor its progress. You must have a trust deed (obtainable from a lawyer, accountant or specialist self-managed super fund administrator), a clear strategy and an annual audit. There are limits on the type of investments the fund can hold. For example, it is not allowed to borrow and investments must be kept at arm's length. If you do not comply with the Superannuation Industry Supervision (SIS) legislation, you may incur steep fines, significantly higher taxation on your fund and, in extreme cases, you may end up in jail.

If you opt for a self-managed fund, the tax office offers a trustee education program and will provide a special booklet. It also aims to contact every self-managed trustee by phone.

As well as having control over where and how your super is invested, your fund can invest in direct shares, for example. These funds offer some useful estate planning and tax planning opportunities, from the tax credits through franked dividends on shares.

One serious concern with self-managed funds is that there is a risk of poor investment strategies, with the possibility of returns lagging behind those reaped by professional managers. They are also expensive to administer. I suggest that you weigh up the pros and cons before setting up a DIY, which ideally will suit couples who have the funds, the time and the necessary financial knowledge.

You should also talk to your accountant or financial adviser for more information on strategies to use with your fund.

Defined benefit and accumulation funds

These are not separate fund types like industry, master and corporate funds; rather, they are different ways of determining the final benefit within the different types of funds. A defined benefit fund sees your final super payout set by a formula created by your employer or the fund rules. It may be a multiple of your final salary (for example, three times) if you retire at 55 and will continue to increase until you reach 65. The benefit of a fund of this type is that you know what you are getting, regardless of the fund's investment performance. On the downside, you really need to be with the company until you retire to gain maximum benefit. With people regularly changing jobs, defined benefit funds have lost much of their attraction.

As a result, accumulation funds have become more attractive to employers. Your employer makes the required contributions, and on termination of your employment you receive this amount, less fees and expenses, along with any earnings made on the fund. You won't know what your final figure will be, but at least you will benefit from the true earnings of the fund. That's why it is so important to take an interest in where your money is invested and to take advantage of any salary sacrifice arrangements offered by your employer.

SEVEN SUPER STRATEGIES

Here are some simple strategies to help boost your retirement funds from going for growth to salary sacrificing.

1 Go for growth

When was the last time you read the superannuation statement sent out by your fund or employer? Did you give it more than a cursory glance? Do you know whether your money is invested in equities or cash? Does your super fund offer member investment choice which allows you to decide on a range of asset classes?

You may find that if you haven't elected to use member investment choice, your money has been invested in a default fund—often the most conservative option. Investing only in cash or another conservative asset class, such as fixed interest, will make it difficult for you to achieve your retirement goals.

Unlike your other investments, you can't spend your super until later in life. A growth asset, such as shares, will give you the maximum nest egg possible because it should deliver a better long-term result.

Jane and her partner, James, had differing views on how to invest their super. Jane was the conservative type and didn't feel comfortable investing in shares. Consequently, she invested her superannuation funds in cash and made no further contributions other than those paid by her employer on her behalf. James, on the other hand, initially chose the growth option, thinking it would be enough to increase his nest egg to enjoy the same standards in retirement as he did now. Thankfully, he crunched the numbers and found that he would need to top up his super fund to achieve his desired lifestyle. Unfortunately, he was unable to persuade Jane to follow suit (see Table 12.2).

Jane invests conservatively

If Jane invests her super conservatively and makes no extra contributions (i.e. relies solely on the SG contributions her employer is making), Table 12.2 shows us that she can expect to have around $356 356 in her super fund when she retires. This sounds like a large amount, but if we allow for the effects of inflation (which erodes away the purchasing power of each dollar over time), then in today's dollars this is only worth around $161 390. This will mean that Jane can expect to have

Table 12.2 James's and Jane's superannuation

	Balance (future $)	Balance (today's $)	Retirement income	% of salary
Jane invests conservatively (SG only)	$356 356	$161 390	$9288	23
James invests for growth (SG only)	$630 382	$285 494	$16 430	41
James invests for growth and adds an extra 7.4% pre tax (on top of his SG)	$1 151 007	$521 280	$30 000	75

Source: BT Financial Group.

Assumptions: SG contributions 9% pa. Conservative return 5.5% pa gross. 1.5% pa management fee. Earnings tax 15%. Inflation is assumed at 2% pa. Retirement income based on payment of benefit as a lifetime pension earning 4.5% pa for a single life male/female aged 65. Jane and James are age 25 and have SG contributed from age 25 until age 65. They are both on a salary of $40 000 pa, which is indexed to inflation each year. Results are shown in today's dollars. The example is based on one set of assumptions and a small change in the assumptions can lead to a large change in results.

an income of only around $9300 a year in retirement. As Table 12.2 reveals, that's slightly less than a quarter of her current income of $40 000.

James invests for growth only

Remember, Jane is investing her super conservatively for twenty years and is in fact only earning a return of 5.5 per cent per annum. On the other hand, James has chosen a growth investment option for his super, such as shares, and earns 8.5 per cent per annum. Investing for growth allows James to retire with around $285 494 in today's dollars. This translates to a retirement income of around $16 400 a year. The chart above shows that investing his super for growth has given James more than $7000 a year more than Jane but he is still only retiring on just over 40 per cent of his previous income.

James invests for growth *and* adds to his super

James decides to make extra contributions of 7.4 per cent to his before-tax salary as a 'salary sacrifice' (see later in this chapter). This amounts to $2960 a year, or $57 a week. If he took this as a cash salary, he would get $39 a week only in his hand after tax at his marginal rate of 31.5 per cent, so it's not a large amount of money for him to give up.

By investing for growth and making regular additional contributions, James ends up with around $521 280 in today's dollars. This translates to an income in retirement of around $30 000 a year. This is around 75 per cent of his pre-retirement income, which is a comfortable standard of living in retirement.

By investing an extra $2960 a year, James retires with about $13 600 extra a year. Making additional contributions during his working lifetime will be of significant benefit to his lifestyle after work.

2 Think long-term

Your super investment is one that can correctly be titled 'long term', since you won't touch it until at least the age of 55. As well as being forced savings for you both, it will allow you the freedom to be more aggressive in your investment choices.

Of course, this will depend entirely on the level of risk you are comfortable with and on your age. If the markets take a tumble and you are heavily weighted towards shares, you should apply the same fundamental rules that you would for your other investments, as discussed in Chapter 9.

If you are nearing retirement age, you may prefer a more conservative strategy. But if you are in your twenties, thirties or forties time is on your side—time for the investment markets to go through their cycles and time for your investments to recover.

3 Make the most of tax benefits

To motivate you to save for your retirement, the government has offered tax savings as an incentive. However, the rules for these tax savings keep changing and some investors are unconvinced that the super environment is tax-friendly enough to justify extra contributions. Others beg to differ.

Here's what happens. If you are an employee, a contributions tax of 15 per cent is paid on your employer's contributions, salary sacrifice contributions and your own tax-deductible contributions when they are paid into your super fund. There may be an additional 15 per cent surcharge on the way in if you are a high-income earner. The surcharge kicks in if you earn more than \$94 691 (2003/04 financial year). For adjusted taxable incomes between \$94 691 and \$114 987, the surcharge phases in at a rate of 1 per cent per \$1399 above \$94 691, but this figure is expected to change. The government is gradually reducing the maximum rate of the surcharge from the original 15 per cent (2002/03 financial year). The maximum rate of surcharge will be further reduced to 13.5 per cent (2004/05) and then 12.5 per cent (2005/06). If you make super contributions from after-tax salary, you will pay neither contributions tax nor the surcharge on those contributions. As of 1 July 2003, the government will match voluntary contributions on a dollar for dollar basis to a maximum of \$1000 for people earning up to \$27 500 and lesser amounts for those earning between \$27 500 and \$40 000.

In addition, your super fund pays tax at a maximum of 15 per cent on all earnings it makes with capital gains taxed at 10 per cent. However, these latter two figures are reason enough to invest in super. The 15 per cent on earnings is much lower than paying tax at a marginal tax rate—as you would with investments outside the super environment. Therefore, your money will grow faster in super because you will have more to start with and you can make the most of compound interest.

When you do reach retirement, you can keep your funds in the super environment through an income stream product such as an allocated pension. The products can allow you to defer or eliminate paying lump sum tax on your retirement benefit and provide you with a tax-effective income stream. However, if you cash in an amount of your super to spend when you retire, you will probably have to pay some tax. Part of the amount you withdraw may be tax-free and the rest will generally be taxed at 16.5 per cent unless your super is worth more than your Reasonable Benefit Limit (see below). For the 2003/04 financial year, the first $117 576 of super is tax-free for people who have reached age 55—this limit is indexed to Average Weekly Ordinary Time Earnings (AWOTE) each 1 July.

What are RBLs?

Reasonable Benefit Limits are the maximum amount of superannuation and termination of employment benefits (eligible termination payments) that individuals can receive over a lifetime at reduced tax rates. For the financial year to 30 June 2004, the lump-sum RBL was $588 056 and, in certain circumstances, you may be eligible for a higher RBL. If you exceed your RBL, you may either lose tax concessions on the excess portion or, if taken in cash, it could be taxed at the top marginal rate.

4 Salary sacrifice

This strategy involves your employer investing a portion of your pre-tax salary into super on your behalf. It will generally only incur a 15 per cent tax, which is probably a lot less than your marginal tax rate. This can mean a significant tax saving if your income is taxed at the highest marginal rate. So, instead of earning income from your traditional investments and paying a higher rate of tax, you can shelter your investments under the superannuation umbrella and at the same time increase your retirement savings. The benefits include:

- a potentially lower income tax rate as your salary is reduced;
- no Fringe Benefits Tax (FBT) on the amount contributed as salary sacrifice;

Table 12.3 Salary sacrifice versus undeducted contributions

Salary sacrifice contributions (before tax)	Undeducted contributions (after tax)
Generally more tax-effective for those on medium to high marginal tax rates	Can be more tax-effective for those on low marginal rates
Employer needs to have an arrangement in place to offer salary sacrifice contributions	You can make after-tax contributions at any time
There are age-based limits on the amount of before-tax contributions that can be made each year (see 'How much money can you put into super?')—page 176	There is no limit on the amount of after-tax contributions
You must be working to make such contributions	Undeducted contributions can be made for a working or a non-working spouse and you may be able to claim a tax offset (see a financial adviser or accountant)

Source: BT Online Website.

- more money working harder for you to compound the benefits;
- forced savings which are automatically deducted.

5 Spouse contributions

This strategy is worth considering if your partner has decided to become a homemaker, is having a baby or is taking some time off work. By continuing to contribute until your spouse is 65, you are taking full advantage of the super environment and its tax benefits for couples.

If your partner earns no more than $10 800 (including Reportable Fringe Benefits) a year and you are prepared to contribute $3000 to their super fund, you will be eligible for a tax offset of $540 a year. If you decide to contribute more than $3000, anything above this amount will not get a tax offset. However, any amount below $3000 will receive a tax offset at a rate of 18 per cent.

You could also be entitled to a part-tax offset (tax rebate) on your contribution if your partner earns more than $10 800 but less than $13 800 a year.

You can also contribute to your partner's super fund regardless of whether they are working or not as long as they are under the age of 65. Of course, in this instance the tax offset is limited, but it is still a smart way to ensure that your combined super nest egg grows as much as possible.

Apart from the ongoing tax break, there is good news on retirement for those couples who split their super. The legislation currently states that when you turn 55, the first $117 576 (for the financial year to 30 June 2004) of the post-June 1983 component of your super is tax free. For couples, this means they can withdraw twice that amount—more than $235 000 of tax-free income.

6 Undeducted contributions

An undeducted contribution is an amount invested in your super fund from your after-tax salary, profits taken from other investments, an inheritance or an amount gifted to you. Because this money is taken from your after-tax salary, there is no tax payable on the contribution and when you retire there is no tax payable on the original amount. The tax advantages are significant because your earnings are taxed at a maximum of 15 per cent in the super fund. However, if you invested outside super, the earnings could be taxed as high as 48.25 per cent.

For example, say you invested an inheritance of $20 000 in your super fund. By the time you retire, the value has grown to $40 000, of which the original $20 000 is tax-free. The $20 000 in earnings you have made will be treated in much the same way as salary sacrifice contributions. That is, there will be a tax-free amount (after you have reached the age of 55) and the remainder will be taxed at a maximum rate of 16.5 per cent, rather than up to 48.5 per cent in a non-super investment.

So should you make an undeducted contribution from your after-tax salary or salary sacrifice from your pre-tax salary? The decision will probably hinge on your marginal tax rate, so it is advisable to check with a financial planner. The features of both strategies are listed in Table 12.3.

7 Consolidate your super

Most of us will change our jobs at least six times during our working life, according to the Australian Bureau of Statistics. This means that both of you potentially have six different super investments in six different super funds, all attracting fees. Consider opening a consolidation account where you can roll over all your super into two personal super fund accounts. The benefits will surprise you.

- You can open a super account for past and future super moneys and still retain your existing super fund with your current employer.
- One account in a fund that suits you best reduces the need to interpret the features and requirements of various super funds.
- A consolidation account eliminates duplication of fees—these add up, even for small amounts.
- All your money is in the one place working harder for you, allowing you to benefit from a more focused investment strategy.

If you have changed jobs in the past ten years, you may not remember where your super is, and you can end up with multiple super funds. It is in your interest to find out. Otherwise you may pay more fees and have less control over your super than you should. Recent statistics suggest there is more than $7 billion in 'lost' super money registered with the government.

To track down missing super, you need to find recent statements with your member number attached. If you can't find any statements, contact past employers and ask them for details of the relevant super funds. If you can't contact a past employer, visit the ATO's Website at www.ato.gov.au or call the ATO on 13 10 20 and ask for the Lost Members' Register. You can complete a form to send to the ATO which will then provide you with details of where your super is held. Armed with this information, some financial institutions offer an additional service by contacting all super funds on your behalf and rolling over your funds for you. All you need to do is complete a rollover authority form. It's a good idea to check the prospectus of your chosen fund for this service before you sign on the dotted line, as it can save you a lot of time.

How much money can you put into super?

You can put in as much as you want to from your after-tax income, but there is an age-based limit on your pre-tax contributions which can be claimed as a tax deduction. This is referred to as your Maximum Deductible Contribution (MDC).

Maximum Deductible Contributions 2003/04

Under 35 years	$13 233
35–49 years	$36 754
50 years and over	$91 149

What if you are self-employed?

If one of you is self-employed, then you may be able to claim the first $5000 of your annual super contributions as a tax deduction. You may then be able to claim a deduction on 75% of the rest of your contributions (up to certain age-based limits), which effectively means you will be investing your before-tax income into super. You will also enjoy the same 15 per cent tax on super fund earnings received by employees.

13

Take cover

Myth: Insurance is a waste of money.
Fact: The worst thing that can happen with insurance is that we never make a claim.

Even though we have a tendency to think we are invincible, at some stage in life most of us will experience trauma—whether it be a death in the family, a car accident, a serious or life-threatening illness or a burglary. That's why protecting your most important assets—your partner and your family—should be a key priority. Think of insurance as a safety net, which can relieve the financial burden when the unexpected happens.

PUT FAMILY FIRST

If you have children or are in a relationship where you have substantial debts, such as a mortgage, it is wise to consider taking out life insurance to cover your partner and/or dependants in the event of your untimely death. By having this form of cover, you will save your partner from having to sell off your assets in order to survive financially.

Take a couple in their mid-thirties who have two school-age children, a \$150 000 mortgage and a \$10 000 car loan. Both are working full-time to meet their weekly commitments. But what if one dies? There will be just one income to do the same job and the risk that, along with a comfortable lifestyle, either the car or home (or both) may have to be sacrificed to meet the debts.

Yet if the couple have taken out a life-insurance policy—based on a lump sum—to take care of the family until the children have finished their education, pay off any debts and provide the surviving partner with money to rebuild their life and plan for the future, the scenario will be quite different.

Before you take out any form of life insurance, you should do your homework, establish which form of insurance will suit you and shop around for the most competitive quote.

You may opt for the more popular—and cheaper—term insurance, which will cover you for a set period of time or until you are aged 65 when the cover will usually cease and you will not receive any benefits. This form of insurance is ideal for a couple, such as the abovementioned case study, who have dependants and steep debts and who will suffer financially as well as emotionally if one dies.

Or there's whole-of-life insurance, which offers life cover plus a savings component to give your policy a cash value you can withdraw or borrow against. However, you pay extra for this type of cover and if you cancel the policy at an early stage you may find your savings have hardly grown. You stop contributing only when you die or when the policy matures at the age of 60 or 65. If you are still alive when the policy matures, you are paid a lump sum; alternatively, there is an agreed payout to the beneficiaries if you die.

Life insurance checklist

- Check your superannuation fund to find out how much life cover it will provide. You may be able to buy extra insurance through a super fund, though it may not be at the most competitive price.
- Look for a flexible policy and read all the fine print.
- Be aware that you get what you pay for.
- Concentrate on the core elements first, then look for added frills.
- An insurance broker can help to find a suitable policy at the right price.
- Ask the broker how many policies they can recommend.
- Remember, cheaper rates apply to non-smokers.
- Disclose everything or risk having the claim rejected.
- Do your best not to under-insure.
- See a financial planner if uncertain about your level or type of cover.
- Visit www.apra.gov.au for a list of life insurance companies.

SAFEGUARD YOUR INCOME

Not everyone needs income protection insurance. But if you are a couple with debts and dependants, it's worth asking yourself a few questions:

- If you are injured or become seriously ill, can you afford to support yourself while off work?
- Will you have enough in the kitty to cover your rent/ mortgage, food and other expenses?
- If you are self-employed with no sick leave, will you be able to support yourself and your family?
- If you're married or in a long-term relationship, will your partner's income be sufficient to cover your costs or will you struggle to pay the bills?

These are just a few of the issues you need to weigh up before seeking the advice of an insurance broker, agent or financial adviser. On the other hand, if your partner earns a good income and you believe you can manage on one salary, you may not even need income protection. This form of insurance is tax-deductible, but any income you receive from the policy is taxable.

Companies will usually insure you for a maximum of 75 per cent of your income. You can choose to be insured up to the age of 65 or for a shorter period. Most policies will also give you a wide choice of waiting periods before the insurance is paid out—with the more expensive kicking in sooner. For example, if you always have enough in the kitty to cover your outgoings for, say, two months, you may opt for a policy that takes effect after 60 days.

The best way to work out how much cover you need is to ask the following question: 'If I were well and truly sick and couldn't work, how much would we need to cover our fixed costs such as housing, schooling, transport and feeding the family?' Remember, you won't need 100 per cent of your salary because your lifestyle will be different. You won't be eating out, buying new work clothes or spending up on entertainment.

It is pointless over-insuring, so you should be realistic about what you need to live on. Income cover of 75 per cent is not a bad amount but if your partner meets most of your living costs, then it may be excessive.

When pricing your premium, insurance companies will look at your health, the nature of your occupation, the length of time you wish to be insured, your income, the percentage of your income you want covered and the waiting period before the payment kicks in.

Income protection can also be purchased with total and permanent disability (TPD) insurance. This means that, if you are unable to work, your monthly income replacement will cease and you will receive a lump-sum TPD payout.

Make sure your income-protection policy is guaranteed renewable—that is, once you have taken out the policy, the insurance company will guarantee to renew it every year regardless of your health—and that increases in the consumer price index (CPI) are built into your package.

While competitively priced, policies often have different features. They range from the basic variety, which replaces a percentage of your income, to policies where features such as nursing assistance are covered.

Most insurance companies have extensive application forms seeking information about your medical history. Most will also ask permission to contact your doctor to confirm your details. You may be required to have a medical. And if you have a particular medical problem, the policy can be written to exclude claims for that condition.

Say you have a bad lower back but are otherwise in good health. Then you can opt for a policy where you will be covered for everything except your lower back, which will help to keep costs down. Of course, you won't be insured against your major risk and you will need to weigh this up when considering your policy.

Before signing, check the fine print as different policies will have different wording for the conditions under which they will pay claims. Some policies pay out only if you are unable to work at all, while others will cover you when you can't perform the duties of your current employment.

An accredited broker can guide you through the maze. While

the process may sound complicated, you will only have to go through it once when you actually buy the policy.

DON'T NEGLECT YOUR HEALTH

Thanks to federal government changes, the pressure is now on to join a private health fund before the age of 30. Otherwise, you will face a 2 per cent loading for every year you delay buying insurance up to the age of 65.

As a couple, taking out private health insurance together has its advantages. It is cheaper than having two single policies and it will automatically cover you if you plan to have a family. Depending on your fund, children are included up until the age of 22 under such a policy. But where do you start?

When Nicole and Shane decided to take out health insurance, they found it was like a matchmaking game. Not only did the policy have to suit their budget, but also their age, state of health, family history and stage of life (married, divorced, etc.).

As a married mother of two young children, Nicole was keen to take out health insurance so the family could have peace of mind, possibly shorter waiting times for non-urgent surgery, their choice of doctor, be covered for private hospital treatment and take advantage of the 30 per cent rebate on premiums paid to a private health fund.

Then there was the pressing matter of age. Both were 29. In Australia, if they were to take out private hospital cover before they turned 30, they would be eligible for the lowest possible 'lifetime health cover' loading. If not, they faced that 2 per cent loading. Nicole described the process:

> If our combined income was more than $100 000 ($50 000 for singles) and we had no hospital cover, we would also be up for a Medicare 1 per cent surcharge. But our combined income was $90 000.
>
> Once we worked out what we wanted, I began contacting the health funds and did some research on the net. We particularly liked the Choice site (www.choice.com.au) and www.iselect.com.au.
>
> In the end, we opted for what I felt was the most economical solution: comprehensive family cover with a high excess. The excess means we have to pay a certain amount if one family member goes into

> hospital, just as you do when claiming on other types of insurance such as car repairs. The higher the excess, the lower our premium would be. We could have also opted for a co-payment option where we pay an agreed amount, say $65 for every day in hospital, each time a service is provided.

As Nicole discovered, provided you do not make many claims, comprehensive family cover plus a high excess can save you money in the long run. What you need to find out is whether the excess is applied every time you go into hospital or on a per year, per membership or per person basis.

With this type of policy, many insurers will also cover your children while they are studying full-time—even into their twenties—or you may be able to pay an extra amount to cover the kids. Depending on the fund, there are also special deals for same-sex couples and single parents with children. Exclusionary policies were another option considered by Nicole and Shane:

> Because we are relatively young, I also looked into buying an exclusionary policy where operations for treatments such as hip and knee replacements are not covered. But during my research I learnt that many health experts caution against this type of product on the basis that you may compromise your health.
>
> My advice is to shop around. Read the fine print and ask about waiting periods for claims or pre-existing conditions and ensure your fund has agreements with your preferred choice of hospital. Before undergoing treatment, contact your fund to find out about extra costs.

There is also the issue of gap cover, which health funds are introducing to bridge the difference between the Medicare scheduled fee and the amount charged by specialists. So you need to find out whether your doctors are part of any of these schemes.

If you wish to take out ancillary cover for treatments such as dental, optical, alternative therapies and physiotherapy, shop around to find out how much you will be insured for each year. And if you are not happy with what's on offer from a fund providing your hospital cover, you can take out ancillary benefits elsewhere.

Struggling with part-time work and two children, Nicole had no desire to fall pregnant again. But if you are an expectant mother and not in a health fund, you will need to rely on the public health system as there is usually a twelve-month waiting period for maternity and obstetrics cover when joining a fund. However, you can easily switch to a family policy so that your baby's health will be covered from birth.

Your health fund has until March each year to adjust its premiums. This is a good time to review your policy. Perhaps your circumstances have changed or you realise your policy does not offer the right features. Feel free to change to another fund but bear in mind that if you're upgrading your cover, you may have to serve out waiting periods for certain benefits.

EASE THE TRAUMA

Unlike income protection, which covers accident or sickness-related injuries that may temporarily prevent you from working, trauma insurance provides cover specifically for more severe illnesses. This type of insurance will provide a lump sum or regular payments to help meet ongoing medical and living expenses in the event of a specified disease or trauma such as cancer, heart surgery, major head trauma, occupationally acquired HIV, multiple sclerosis or loss of a limb, to name a few. The range of conditions will vary widely depending on the policy you select.

The benefit of trauma insurance is that payments are made when your diagnosis is confirmed by a doctor rather than on your death. This will help relieve your family of additional financial pressures when they need it the most.

You may not think a serious illness will happen to you, but the statistics are stacking up against us. For example, the risk of some form of coronary heart disease for a 40-year-old is one in two for men and one in three for women. For cancer, one in three men and one in four women will be directly affected before age 75.

> I heard some sad news recently about an old friend. She and her husband were in their late thirties and had recently had

a long-awaited baby girl through the IVF program. Three months after the birth, she was breastfeeding and discovered a lump that she thought was just a blocked milk duct. She left it for another six months before finally visiting her GP. The news was devastating. She had breast cancer and was operated on immediately. She had mistakenly thought that she was immune to breast cancer if she breastfed.

With a baby on the way, the couple had reviewed their insurance cover to make sure that they were fully covered for any situation. Luckily, they had taken out trauma insurance as there was a history of cancer in her family.

Any serious illness will have an emotional effect on the family but, if uninsured, it can have a profound financial effect as well. For my friend, the surgery was successful but she had to wait several months before returning to work. During that time, she was unable to do even the most basic of tasks at home, such as clean the house, bath the baby or walk the dog. So the family required child care and a part-time housekeeper. These expenses were met through their trauma policy, which helped them cope until she was fit enough to go back to work.

CONTENTS COUNT

One in six of Australia's 7.4 million homes are not covered by building or home contents insurance, according to research by NRMA Insurance. This represents 414 000 home owners and 866 000 people who rent their homes. To put it into perspective, it is equivalent to the population of Perth having no home insurance cover.

To protect your assets, it's essential to not only take out full contents replacement insurance but to update it every year. You also need to make sure you aren't under-insured on big-ticket items so you won't be out of pocket in the event of a burglary, fire or other unforeseen disaster.

To find out whether you are adequately insured, complete the NRMA Insurance checklist on page 186. Suggested replacement costs are in brackets. Items marked with an asterisk have limits to their cover under general contents insurance. Contact your insurer for details. Then add up each sub-total to calculate the total cost of replacing your household contents in the event of loss.

THE LITTLE EXTRAS

Along with your home contents policy, you may want to take out extra cover for jewellery and domestic workers' compensation. Take the case of Natalie and Jason, who were under the false assumption that their jewellery was covered by their home contents policy. That was until a friend pointed out to them that all of their jewellery was covered for a maximum of $1000 only, an amount that wouldn't replace their wedding bands, let alone Natalie's diamond engagement ring.

So when their insurance policy came up for renewal, they took the time to read all the documents that accompanied it. The jewellery details were there in black and white, as was an item about domestic workers' compensation, which would cover them in the event they were at fault for an injury to their home cleaner.

Natalie picked up the phone to clarify a few issues with their insurer. For a flat annual fee of $25, the domestic workers' compensation provided cover of up to $10 million. What a bargain, she thought.

But what of her jewellery? She was told they could specify items, such as an engagement ring, within their policy. Any jewellery items in excess of $1000 required a certificate of valuation—not more than five years old and in Australian currency. They would also face a premium.

If she were wearing her wedding and engagement ring all the time, it was wiser to insure them as specified portable valuables so they would be covered within and outside the home. For this, there was an additional premium and the insurer would need to know the replacement value.

In weighing up whether to increase your premium, remember that the worst thing that can happen with insurance is that you *never* make a claim.

NRMA Insurance checklist

Household goods, including:

Washing machine and clothes dryer	$1500
Vacuum, heaters and fans	$1000
Sewing machine and overlocker	$1200
Food and alcohol	$1200
Kitchen appliances	$1500
Dishwasher and microwave	$1500
Fridge and freezer	$1500
Saucepans, ovenware, plastic containers, etc.	$1500
Dinner sets, glassware, cutlery	$2000
Items containing gold or silver up to	$2500*

Sub-total: $.........................

Furniture, including:

Lounge suite, coffee tables, wall units and bookcases	$6500
Dining table, chairs, sideboards, display units	$4500
Beds	$3500
Wardrobe, dressing table, drawers	$2000
Desks and chairs	$1000
Indoor pot plants, aquarium, etc.	$1000

Sub-total: $.........................

Fittings and furnishings, including:

Wall-to-wall carpets	$6500
Rugs, floor coverings	$3000
Curtains, cushions, blinds	$5500
Pictures, mirrors, photos	$2000
Lamps, light fittings	$2000
Ornaments, vases and clocks	$2000
Works of art up to	$2500*
Curios up to	$2500*

Sub-total: $.........................

Linen and manchester, including:

Towels and sheets	$1500
Quilts, blankets, bedspreads, pillows	$1500
Electric blanket, underlays	$ 800

Sub-total: $.........................

Clothing and personal items, including:	
Clothes, shoes	$6000 (per adult)
	$3000 (per child)
Luggage, handbags and wallets	$1000
Hairdryers, shavers, toiletries	$ 800
Makeup, perfumes and colognes	$1000
Jewellery up to	$1000*
Watches up to	$1000*

Sub-total: $...........................

Entertainment and hobbies, including:	
Television, stereo system, CD/VCR/DVD players	$3200
Computer, printer, fax, related equipment	$6000
Cameras, video and film equipment	$4500
Musical instruments, music	$1000
Toys, games, books, hobby items	$3000
CDs, DVDs, tapes, records, computer game cartridges and discs up to	$2500
Stamps, medals up to	$2500*
Coin, card collections up to	$2500*

Sub-total: $...........................

Outdoor and tools, including:	
Portable garden shed	$ 800
Lawn mower, hoses, garden tools	$2000
DIY tools, drills, hammers	$2600
Barbecue, outdoor furniture	$2000
Portable swimming pools, swings	$4000
Bicycles, sporting and exercise equipment	$2000
Garden lights, spotlights	$1000
Tools of trade up to	$1000*

Sub-total: $...........................

TOTAL: $...........................

14

Where there's a will . . .

Myth: We don't need a will because everything will go to the family.

Fact: If you die without a will, otherwise known as intestate, your estate will be divided according to law.

Making a will is a simple, inexpensive task, but it is one neglected by an average of 30 per cent of Australians who die each year. The younger you go, the higher the statistics: 96 per cent of people in their twenties do not have a will, while 60 per cent in their thirties have not put pen to paper to determine who will get what in the event of their untimely death. Perhaps they find the idea of facing up to their mortality too confronting, or maybe they simply never get around to doing it. New South Wales Acting Public Trustee Peter Whitehead points out:

> When you are looking at couples in their thirties, they're at a vulnerable stage in their lives. It's a time when they need to set up structures because they could have dependants or they could have complex arrangements such as a mortgage, superannuation, credit card debts, life insurance or maybe no life insurance. By sitting down and writing their wills together, they can actually address their net assets and debts, do some general life planning and make sure they look after the ones who matter to them most when they're gone.

If you're still not convinced about the benefits of making a will, consider this: If you die intestate, your estate may lose opportunities for saving tax. After a lifetime of paying taxes, this is probably the last thing you would want.

WHO SHOULD MAKE A WILL?

Anyone who has assets, is getting married, entering a de facto or same-sex relationship, having a child, getting divorced or is aged over eighteen with possessions they want a particular party to have should make a will. For these people, a will should be top of the must-do list, right up there with savings, investment and superannuation. Otherwise, if you die without a will, your assets may end up with people you may not choose—or the government if you have no relatives closer than cousins.

You should alter your will each time your circumstances in life change, such as divorce, remarriage, the birth of children or grandchildren, death of your executor or beneficiaries, or the purchase of property. That way you can ensure your true wishes will be carried out.

If you have dependant children, there is the big concern of who will look after them now and in the future and how their upbringing will be financed. A well-prepared will with a nominated guardian, life insurance and superannuation should enable you to provide adequately for their long-term emotional and financial welfare.

HOW TO MAKE A WILL

You can either have a solicitor draw up your wills, visit the public trustees office in your state, buy a do-it-yourself kit from a newsagent or stationer or download documents from the Internet. Since a will is so important, the safest bet is to use the services of an expert, particularly if children are involved. This should safeguard you against any misinterpretation and you will receive advice on the most appropriate form of the will together with a better understanding of how it can meet your estate-planning requirements.

A DIY kit is a feasible alternative provided you are disciplined and your affairs are straightforward. But if your estate or family structure is more complex and you are not the most reliable person when it comes to filling in forms, the DIY kit may languish under a pile of papers uncompleted, even unopened.

A valid will should be in writing, typed or handwritten and signed by yourself and two witnesses who are not beneficiaries or the spouses of beneficiaries. In your wills, you should appoint a person or people you trust to administer your estate as your executors, name a guardian if you have any children, and name your beneficiaries and which part of your estate you wish them to inherit.

There are several issues that must be considered, some of which may require expert advice. For instance, be aware that if you decide to leave your place of residence to one child and a holiday house or investment property to another, the latter can incur capital gains tax when the property is sold.

WHAT HAPPENS IF YOU DIE WITHOUT A WILL?

Each state has variations of what happens to your estate if you die without a will. In Queensland, for example, if you die without a will and are married with no children, your estate will automatically go to your spouse. If there are children and the estate is worth more than $150 000, the spouse will receive the first $150 000 plus household goods and an opportunity to keep the family home, with the remainder split among the children and spouse according to the *Succession Act*.

If there is no spouse, the children receive an equal share. If there is no spouse and no children, the parents of the deceased are left the proceeds. If there are no parents, relatives follow. If there are no relatives closer than cousins, the estate will go to the state government.

HOW TO CHOOSE AN EXECUTOR

I knew a solicitor who took more than nine months to wind up his brother's estate . . . and he knew what he was doing! In choosing an executor, it is important to appoint someone who has the ability to administer your estate (see Table 14.1), which will involve dealing with solicitors, organising probate, tax issues, liaising with real estate agents, negotiating offers on property, consoling grieving relatives and generally being accountable for your decisions. As Peter Whitehead says:

> As an executor, if you make the wrong decisions, you can be answerable to the beneficiaries. That's why people should choose someone who can facilitate expert advice with confidence—not just a friend or relative you admire or respect. To avoid a conflict of interest, they would also be wise to appoint an executor who is not a beneficiary. Otherwise, if there is a dispute, will they be able to wear two hats—as a beneficiary and an executor—to defend a claim that has been brought against the estate by another member of the family?

Be aware that if you have appointed a member of your family to be the executor and trustee of long-term trusts for your children, they may have to look after the personal needs of your children as well as the financial management of the trust. This may be an onerous task for one person.

Aside from friends and relatives, there are other options for appointing an executor. Some people appoint their solicitor, while others prefer a public trustee who specialises in will-making and administering estates and trusts.

THE COST OF A WILL

Costs vary according to the complexity of the will. A basic will drawn up by a solicitor may set you back as little as $200, while more complex documents may cost up to $800. A will that involves special trusts can blow out to $4000.

If you are using the public trustee to draw up your wills, costs will vary from state to state. For example, in Victoria a couple wil pay $195 for two wills through the public trustee, in Queensland it's a free service while in New South Wales the public trustee does not charge to make a will provided you appoint it as executor or co-executor with your spouse or partner.

Table 14.1 Don't leave your best friend to chart their way through this

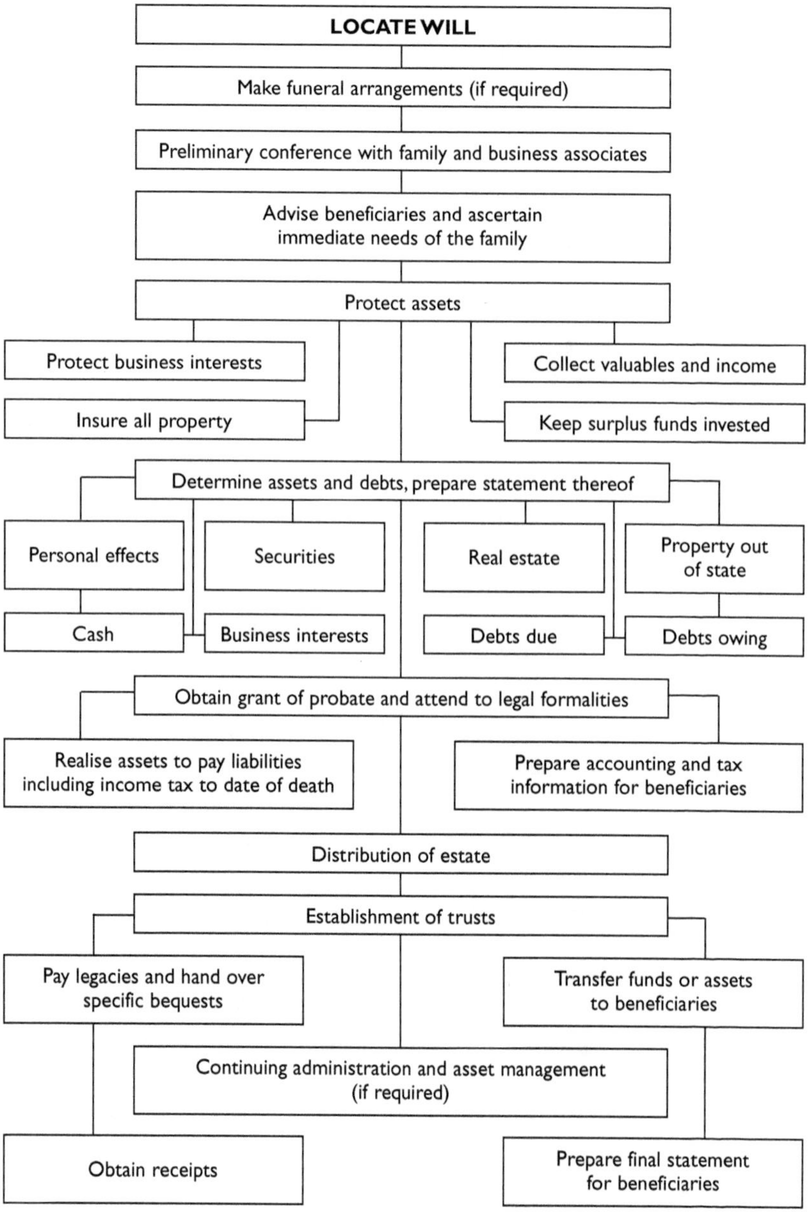

Source: Looking After Your Life's Work is Our Work, Public Trustee NSW

If you appoint the public trustee as executor, costs will also vary and will depend on the complexity of your assets and your wills. It is best to contact your nearest public trustee's office to discuss how the law operates.

Solicitors, in comparison, charge the executor for obtaining a grant of probate then on an hourly basis for whatever the executor wants them to do. Probate is an order given by the Supreme Court stating that this is the last will of the deceased. It allows the executor to collect and distribute the estate according to the will.

WHAT REVOKES A WILL?

Usually, when you make a will, you revoke all previous wills. Marriage will also revoke a will unless it has been made in contemplation of the marriage. Divorce revokes the part of the will that deals with the partner you are divorcing. For example, if a husband leaves half of his estate to his parents and half to his wife, and they divorce, the gift to the wife is revoked and is treated as if she did not exist at the date of death. There may be slight variations in this law depending on which state you reside in when you die.

A pre-nuptial or binding financial agreement can supersede the conditions in your will. If you have such a document, bring this to the attention of the will-maker.

THE TAX BENEFITS OF TRUSTS

Setting up a testamentary trust for your children can reap tax benefits. And, depending on the size of your estate, this can amount to considerable savings. Say, for instance, you have set aside $150 000 to set up three trusts for three children at $50 000 each. Under such a trust, the first $6000 of income earned is tax-free. This is extra money you can use for your children's education or future needs.

You can also set out the terms under which they can access the funds after your death. Many people, including grandparents, use trusts to provide benefits for children in their wills.

As the trusts can continue for some time, the choice of trustee is important—experience in prudential funds management is a key skill.

WHO CAN CONTEST A WILL?

In some states, spouses, former spouses (including de facto and same-sex partners), children and any person (relative or not) who has lived in the household and who can prove they have been dependent on the deceased can contest a will. Those contesting the will have to show they are in financial need.

For example, a widow dies in a car accident without leaving a will. Under intestate laws in New South Wales, for example, the estate is distributed to her sisters. However, she has two stepchildren who she brought up as her own but never adopted. They make a claim on the basis of financial need and are awarded a portion of the estate. If a will had been made, all parties may have been spared considerable emotional angst, not to mention legal costs.

A will can also be contested on the grounds that the deceased did not have the mental capacity to prepare a will or that their thought processes were affected by undue influence or duress.

WHERE TO KEEP YOUR WILL

Grieving families spend a lot of time trying to track down wills. It's best to keep your will somewhere safe and, if appointing a private executor, make sure you give them a copy because they have to activate it when you die. Or, at the very least, tell them where it is, make it somewhere accessible and give them an understanding of what's in your estate.

DE FACTO AND SAME-SEX COUPLES

Different states take a variety of approaches as to how de facto and same-sex relationships affect inheritance without a will. For instance, in Victoria, same-sex couples are recognised by law so if they move in together and accumulate assets—and if either of them dies intestate—they can then make a claim on the estate. In New South Wales, a same-sex partner and a de facto spouse can inherit the same proportion of an estate that a legal spouse would inherit if they meet certain conditions about the nature and quality of their relationship. This can be affected by the existence of other next of kin such as children or a separated spouse. In South Australia, same-sex couples are currently not recognised and de factos must prove to the court they were in a relationship with the deceased for at least five years. In Tasmania, same-sex couples are also not recognised while de factos need to meet certain criteria. Many states are reviewing their laws on this issue. If in doubt, check with your solicitor.

THE LAW PREVAILS

Two women fell madly in love and one moved into the other's home, a three-bedroom waterfront apartment in Melbourne. Tragically, two-and-a-half years later, the partner who owned the property died of a heart condition. There was no will, so her girlfriend inherited the apartment. Her parents, who had met the girlfriend only once, did not approve of the relationship and contested the will, but received nothing. Peter Whitehead says:

> This type of scenario is becoming more common as an increasing number of couples—heterosexual and same-sex—move in and out of relationships. They may be in a relationship but because it is early on they may not necessarily want their estate to pass to their new partner. They may want their parents and siblings to get something, but without a will the law prevails.
>
> People should make sure that once they are in a relationship and have assets that they have a will. Even if you don't have many assets, the emotional side can be difficult to manage. I have had people's relatives ring up and say that they have big issues about CD collections and furniture that a same-sex partner is getting when they think they should have them.

THE FINAL WORD

The final word on wills comes from Tim Whitney, succession partner with Brisbane legal firm McCullough Robertson: 'If you want to have fighting kids not speaking to each other and their children growing up not knowing who their cousins are, then don't resolve arguments, don't make a decent will, don't realise the will is the most important document you will ever sign because it just doesn't wind up your life's work, it is one of the main things you can use to keep your family still ringing each other up at Christmas time.'

A cautionary tale

It's best to take legal advice on how to purchase property to avoid unnecessary trauma in the event of untimely death. This was certainly so in a case involving two siblings who were left with nothing when their mother died suddenly.

In her forties, she had recently remarried and had used her savings to buy a home as 'joint tenant' with her much older—and much poorer—second husband. Under joint tenancy laws, her share went to her surviving spouse regardless of the terms of her will.

But if the mother had bought the house as 'tenant in common', she could have left her share to her children in her will. And she could have made a provision for 'a lifetime interest' in the home so that her husband could have remained there until his death.

15

When love goes wrong

Myth: There are ways to hide your assets from the Family Court.

Fact: The Family Court is a 'show and tell' regime and takes a tough stance if you're caught hiding assets.

Along with the current desire for instant gratification, we seem to be living in an age where we believe nothing is forever. All the statistics tell us we have fallen out of love with marriage, as more than 42 per cent of marriages now end in divorce, according to the Institute of Family Studies.

Some might argue that couples don't try hard enough anymore. Whatever the reasons, we are more wary of taking the plunge into marriage and are opting to live together first. According to the Australian Bureau of Statistics, 72 per cent of couples now prefer to live together before marriage, compared with 31 per cent back in 1981.

Society has helped ease the pressure. It is not uncommon these days for couples to have had one or two serious de facto relationships before tying the knot, with some couples choosing not to marry at all. But still it seems that, whether you are married or living as a de facto couple, many relationships still struggle to survive in the long term.

Divorce is a part of our lives, with blended families and 'exes' everywhere you turn. Dealing with the emotional side is tough enough, but the financial side also needs the right care and attention. Otherwise, one party may find themselves not only distraught but out of pocket too.

Many people may need to have an ongoing relationship in one form or another if there are children involved. So whether you are a de facto, same-sex or married couple in the throes of separation, the first step is to take the time to deal with the emotions then sit down with your partner and try to logically deal with the issues. If mediation is necessary, then get some.

If you're about to untie the knot, it's vital to take a few steps to make sure the financial outcome is fair to both parties. Staying calm, being honest about your assets, seeking professional advice and thinking smart are all essential if you are to avoid an ugly ending.

HEAL YOUR HEART

Often in a divorce, which can be applied for after twelve months of separation, one party may be more devastated than the other. While one may already be moving on, the other may be left bewildered, bitter, hurt and resentful. If your heart is broken and you are struggling to get through the day, this is not the time to be making decisions that will affect the rest of your life.

To help make the right financial decisions, you need to be in sound emotional, mental and physical shape. A counsellor can assist you to get over the split, adjust to your new single status and help you to move on so that you can establish other relationships. Contact an organisation such as Relationships Australia (www.relationships.com.au) to meet a qualified counsellor who will discuss your concerns and provide you with coping mechanisms.

SEEK ADVICE

Make a list of your assets and liabilities, then contact a competent solicitor to find out your rights, obligations, costs and entitlements.

Good divorce lawyers will look at ways to resolve rather than inflame any dispute. They will talk about mediation and negotiation rather than marching straight into a courtroom. They will advise you not to lie to each other and try to remain calm in order to reach a fair and equitable agreement. They can also help with issues of child support and shared parenting. If necessary, they can further advise on issues such as apprehended violence orders if there is a history of physical abuse.

An accountant can help to restructure your finances and inform you of issues such as any capital gains tax implications if you have to sell assets other than the family home.

HONESTY IS THE BEST POLICY

If you are splitting up, it's essential to be upfront about all your assets, as 'nothing spoils a sensible resolution of property faster than a lie', warns Robert Benjamin, an accredited family law specialist at Watts McCray. 'If one party finds the other is telling a lie, that can cause a complete change of heart. This also applies to non-disclosure of assets rather than simply poor disclosure.'

Make a completely honest list of your assets and liabilities. If one party values a home at $1 million, while the other is convinced it's worth $1.5 million, save further heartache by organising a joint valuation. The same applies to valuables such as jewellery. But bear in mind that secondhand jewellery may not fetch anywhere near its retail value. Benjamin says that in some courts the approach is hide-and-seek. But the Family Court and the Federal Magistrates Court of Family Law are a show-and-tell regime. If you hide assets and get caught, the court will adopt a very tough attitude in terms of what you want and a very sympathetic attitude in terms of what your partner wants. So there are huge inducements to be frank and upfront about disclosing your assets.

In one case that came before the Family Court, a husband swore in his affidavit that his income and assets were a certain amount. He wanted a property split of 60–40 in his wife's favour because he was earning good money and they had two children who were in her care.

However, the wife was after an 80–20 split as she felt her contribution was greater because of the children. And her lawyer was armed with a little black receipt book which revealed a much higher income than the husband had declared.

The result? The court took a dim view of the husband's dishonesty and ruled in favour of his wife. It also decided he should pay her costs. Undeterred, the husband appealed against the decision but the appeals court ruled that, since he had plotted to hide his assets and play cute, his case was dismissed—again with an order for costs.

With family businesses, people often attempt to hide hard-to-detect assets, according to Benjamin:

> They tend to try to diminish the value of their business. And it's hard sometimes to work out if the business is going downhill because they're siphoning the money off elsewhere or whether it's going downhill because they're mourning the loss of their relationship.
>
> It's one of those or sometimes a combination. Often you'll put accountants into their firms and discover that some of the overheads, like the running of a car, is in fact the girlfriend or boyfriend's car and that the rent isn't just for the factory. It's for the home unit in town for the lover.

The hard part is to tell people to be honest with the Tax Office, Benjamin says. One party may have fudged their income, understating it by $20 000 a year:

> My advice is to go back to your accountant and tell them to lodge amended tax returns for a couple of reasons. First, if you tell the Tax Department of your error rather than allowing them to catch you, you're far better off. Second, you'll know what your liabilities are. Third, when you go to court, you'll know what the property pool is. If you don't, you may end up in court and get caught for not declaring income. You will then get thumped by the court and the tax department will probably come in afterwards and clean up whatever is left over.

PUT FINANCES FIRST

The period straight after a break-up is usually the most traumatic, with once-loving couples left fighting for a fair share of their joint assets while still coming to terms with their shattered lives.

Even though you may not feel like it, you do need to take some action—and quickly—to protect your share of any money, particularly if you have a joint savings or cheque account requiring just one signature. Otherwise, the wounded party may embark on a withdrawal program that could leave you struggling to pay for a bus fare.

If you have joint accounts, contact your financial institution and put a request in writing to ensure two signatures are required to withdraw funds. It is also vital to prevent any further debts from credit or store cards held in both names. Contact the card provider as soon as possible so that you are not left with any liability if your separated partner opts for some serious retail therapy. Failure to do this may mean you will be liable for the debt along with interest charges on any outstanding amount. But if the card is in your partner's name only, you will not be liable.

If you have a redraw facility attached to your mortgage, check with your provider to make sure that the amount cannot be increased unless there are two signatures. Then contact a solicitor to ensure any property held in both names cannot be sold without your knowledge. At the same time, discuss drawing up a new will.

CHANGE YOUR PRIORITIES

Often a divorce can mean a drastic change in lifestyle. Rather than dwell on the negatives, use this time to revisit your budget and re-think your priorities. Perhaps you were never really happy in your home and it will serve only to remind you of the past.

If you like the neighbourhood, you can always downsize to something more affordable. If need be, look at other schooling, holiday, car and clothing options. A financial counsellor can help you hone your budget and devise appropriate strategies.

DIVORCE ALTERNATIVES

Do-it-yourself

If you have few assets, you are both in agreement with who gets what, and there aren't children involved, then doing it yourself can be a cheap, sensible alternative. You can even prepare your divorce online at www.familycourt.gov.au—just follow the prompts. However, if you have property that needs to be transferred, then stamp duty and other tax issues may be a complicating factor so seeking professional help is probably a better option.

Online settlement

Some couples find that they just can't agree on a settlement but don't want to spend hours in court and big bucks on legal fees. Don't despair. There is help available. Websites such as www.settlementonlinesystems.com.au provide a secure, quick and cost-efficient means of reaching a settlement within your limits by providing a confidential, password-protected, automated dispute-resolution service. You simply each pay $100 and the system acts as a go-between.

One party needs to complete a registration form and the system will then contact the other party to begin the resolution process. All bids for settlement are confidential—neither party knows what the other has submitted. If the two offers are within a third of each other, the difference is halved and agreement is made. It's all done via email and is legally binding so you can take it to the Family Court for approval.

If you find that you are still unsuccessful in reaching an agreement, you could try www.mediateonline.com.au. This service provides an independent mediator either online or in person to help you resolve your differences. Nothing discussed or agreed on can be used against you in court. The process starts with a mediator explaining the ground rules. Each party is then able to state their case, with or without a solicitor, and this is followed by a joint discussion. You are then able to privately discuss any issues with the mediator. The final joint discussion will hopefully provide agreement on the way forward.

IF YOU GO TO COURT

If you are unable to agree on a settlement and there is so much bitterness that mediation is not an option, you may have to go to court.

If you are married, in a same-sex or de facto relationship and you have children, your case is governed under the federal *Family Law Act*. Issues such as maintenance, or where the children will live, fall under federal law until they reach the age of eighteen.

If, however, there is a question mark about whether they have been cared for properly, the case is dealt with by various state authorities. If one party is attempting to gain custody (residence), the case will be determined by either the Family Court or the Federal Magistrates Court—both under the umbrella of the *Family Law Act*.

PROPERTY SETTLEMENTS

A three-stage process is used to handle cases of separation that come before the courts under Australia's *Family Law Act*.

First, a court looks at the total assets, including property and any investments in shares, managed funds, trusts, lottery wins, and so on. Until recently, superannuation was not included as part of the property settlement. But since 28 December 2002, it has been regarded as property and can also be split.

Second, the court notes where the money came from and who contributed to earning it. Say, for example, one partner's mother dies shortly after separation and leaves an inheritance. The court will still value this as a part of matrimonial property, but it may be argued that the other partner's contribution is only small. The court will also look at how much each side brought to the partnership from the day they commenced the relationship, not necessarily the date of marriage. And it will consider non-financial contributions, such as child care and household costs.

Third, under family law, future needs are taken into consideration. If one party has spent a significant amount of time caring for the family, has lost the capacity to earn an income and is still required to care for young children, the courts can award an additional amount depending on a variety of individual factors.

Once an agreement has been reached on who gets what, settlement can be handled in one of two ways. The first is by court order, which can be beneficial if there is any transfer of assets, as this provides for capital gains tax rollover relief. Put simply, it means the assets are transferred into the new name without incurring any capital gains tax. It also means that there will probably not be any stamp duty payable.

The second method is with a binding financial agreement, which can be made by both parties and their solicitors and does not need to go through the courts. This process provides stamp duty relief, but not capital gains tax relief. You need to do the sums on both scenarios, preferably with an accountant. But generally, if you are transferring only a car or home, it may be a better solution.

If you have other assets, it may be worthwhile for both parties to meet their respective solicitors and accountants to discuss any potential tax liabilities so that all relevant matters are covered and agreed on at the one time. For example, say you agree as part of your settlement to take over an investment property you bought together. By doing so, you also agree to a reduced share of other assets. Yet, when you come to sell this property in order to maintain your lifestyle, you will have to pay capital gains tax. If you don't seek professional advice, you may find you take over an asset that will come back to bite you down the track.

THE COST OF GOING TO COURT

Smart couples about to go their separate ways should do everything in their power to agree on a settlement before resorting to the courts. Tools such as those described earlier should be the first option. If you don't want a lawyer to be the biggest financial winner, swallow your pride and talk to your partner.

The cost of going to court can be frightening, Benjamin says:

> There are two courts in property proceedings—the Federal Magistrates Court and the Family Court. A three-day case in the Family Court can be anywhere between $30 000 and $50 000 each in costs. This covers the barristers' and solicitors' fees and valuations on the home, the superannuation fund, furniture and car. Sometimes you'll need a report from experts about where the kids are going to live and when you put all that together it is an enormous amount. If you are arguing over $10 million, it may be a worthwhile exercise to go to court. But if you are arguing over $200 000 or $300 000, it makes much more sense to use mediation where possible.

The amount of property you jointly own will determine which court you use. If the value of your assets is more than $700000, the case will be heard in the Family Court. If it is less then it goes to the Federal Magistrates Court, where cases tend to run for about two days and usually cost about half as much as the Family Court. That's because the nature of disputes is often narrower. With superannuation now included in divorce settlements, more cases will fall into the realm of the Family Court. Benjamin explains that the Family Court values highly those parties who are realistic from the start. If one party makes a sensible and reasonable offer and the other a ridiculous offer and wastes the court's time then the court may demand that the unrealistic party pays for all the court costs if it can be proven that the initial 'reasonable' offer was rejected.

After all, if there are young children involved, couples will need to be in constant communication for a long time. So it helps if they will be able to meet without wanting to inflict serious bodily harm on each other!

TIMING THE SETTLEMENT

The view of most mediators and counsellors is that the earlier the settlement, the better. In reality, there will often be one partner who has been thinking about a breakup for a long time and has gone through the motions a thousand times in their mind. They will have gone through the various stages of emotional recovery before the shock announcement and will be ready to move on. But the other may have had little or no idea that there was a problem, particularly if their partner has been unfaithful.

Often the person who initiates the separation has a conscience problem and can sacrifice too much to ease their guilt. Say the wife has been having an affair. She may be likely to demand less because she perceives she has been the guilty party. Whereas if the wife were to catch the husband having an affair, she may well wish to punish him because she saw the marriage as being a good relationship and the husband as the one who spoilt it.

Most experts agree that a reasonable time—say a couple of months—needs to pass before the issue of property settlement is discussed so that one party doesn't feel railroaded by the other. It's not necessary to wait until the divorce is finalised, but it's a good idea to give both parties time to come to terms with what has happened so that they can deal with it in a calm and reasonable frame of mind.

The advantages of dealing with property issues within a reasonable timeframe is that you can possibly avoid going to court and all the heartache that goes with it. You can focus on the future and not on litigation, which by its nature forces people to focus on the past. An early settlement may also allow the development of a new relationship.

SETTLE OUT OF COURT

Aside from the costs—both financial and emotional—there are several other good reasons for separating couples to settle out of court. In the process of negotiating a settlement, it pays to remember that by going to court, the number of good results that can be achieved is narrowed.

For example, if you are on good terms, you may be able to ask permission of the other party to retain a mortgage on the home for three or four years so that you can re-establish yourself financially.

You may be able to delay the sale of a property until the kids finish their schooling. Or you may be able to leave a mortgage over a property so that you can continue to run a business, but give the other party a charge back over the business with a scheme to reduce the mortgage over time.

You can initiate all these options outside the court system. Of course, it is hard to keep emotions out of it, particularly if there is another party involved or if one partner is feeling hurt, alienated or betrayed.

The real art is to get people to focus on the problems, not beating each other up. That's where a good family lawyer comes in handy. 'Sometimes it's almost worth saying to your client, "Go in there and let him or her say what they're going to say and acknowledge that it's said",' Benjamin says. 'I think a lot of people go to court not for the money or for the result but because they want to say something to the other party.'

THE DE FACTO FACTOR

Living together seems to be a much more attractive option for couples these days than walking down the aisle. Perhaps it's the high divorce rate, which suggests that society places less importance on that piece of paper. However, there are still some anomalies in the law.

If you are in a heterosexual or same-sex partnership and have been living as a de facto couple for the required amount of years before separation, any property is adjusted under the relevant state acts covering de facto relationships. Essentially, the pool of assets and the issue of contributions are examined. But there are key differences. Superannuation is currently not included and future needs are not taken into account when calculating the value of any property.

Let's look at Heather and Julian. Heather has no children and has never married, but has been in two long-term relationships. She also has few assets in her name. Her partner, Julian, has moved on from a divorce six years ago and has continued to build his wealth. They meet and decide to move in as a de facto couple, renting a house together. They then have two children in quick succession. Unfortunately, the relationship sours and they don't make it past four years as a partnership.

Because they were not married, Julian is not obliged to part with any of his superannuation or provide for Heather's future needs as the mother of his two children. The court looks at Heather's contribution as a partner and mother and what she has brought into the relationship and awards her a small amount of Julian's assets.

He, of course, is still required to pay maintenance for the children. However, if they had been married it would have been a different story. Julian would have had to include his superannuation in the property pool and Heather's future needs would have been taken care of as well.

Fortunately for Heather, Julian is a caring man and provides an additional payment to assist her. But not everyone is like Julian.

If there are no children involved, the rights of a de facto spouse in New South Wales, for example, resemble those of a married couple, provided you have lived together for the required period. You may have the same rights to social security benefits as legally married spouses and if you have a child you are entitled to child support from the other parent. You can also make a claim on any funds in a company owned by your partner.

Applications for property division are made to the Supreme Court, District Court or the Local Court within two years of the end of a relationship. Where the case is heard will depend on the size of the assets and where the parties live. For assets of less than $750 000, the matter will be heard in the District Court. Anything higher goes to the Supreme Court, where costs are usually about half that of the Family Court. This varies from state to state.

In splitting property, a court will consider both financial and non-financial contributions—that is, how much one half has contributed in the form of labour for renovating or answering phones for business purposes, for example—and the contribution of each as a parent and homemaker.

Putting property in joint names is preferable for de facto couples because it implies joint activity. One partner will then have to persuade a court against splitting the assets equally. It all comes down to contributions at the start and during the relationship.

One tricky issue is the non-financial contributions of a homemaker. Take the case of Victorian couple Alison and Simon, whose live-in relationship lasted just eighteen months, six months short of the period required by the *Family Law Act* to be classed as de facto. They bought a home together, but it was in his name. While he paid the mortgage, she toiled to renovate the property by herself. They also had a joint account that required just one signature to withdraw money. And unfortunately their split was acrimonious.

Simon did not want to give Alison one cent from the sale of the property, despite her role in refurbishing the house. He argued that he had made all the mortgage payments and financed the renovation. He also withdrew all the money from their joint bank account. Benjamin comments:

> Alison is in real trouble. You have to be in a de facto relationship for two years before you can make a claim. There are some special circumstances—for example, if they had a child. But she is starting behind the eight ball because they moved in for only eighteen months. She could go to court and say how much she contributed but it will be a difficult, high-risk claim. If she goes to the Equity Court because the two years is not up, she has to really show what she has done to improve that property.
>
> One big problem is that, while improvements to a house may make the property look nice, they may not preserve or increase its value. If the court rules against her, she could also end up with a cost order.

If the home had been in joint names, Benjamin says, Alison would have been in a better position to argue her case for a share of the property and any other assets. She could have argued that it was a gift while Simon would have a tough time getting more than 50 per cent because he would have to prove she had been holding it 'on trust' for him.

Alison's best option now is to take sound legal advice then sit down with her ex-partner to negotiate a settlement.

CALCULATING CHILD SUPPORT

Child support payments are set by an administrative formula amounting to a percentage of gross income less an annual living allowance of about $12 000. For the first child, the rate is 18 per cent, for two children it is 27 per cent and for three children it is 32 per cent. It continues to rise with subsequent children. So if you're earning $62 000 gross a year, minus $12 000 for the living allowance, the formula is applied to the remaining $50 000. If your ex is earning income of more than $29 000 a year, this will also be taken into account. The complex formula can be varied through the Child Support Agency if you are unhappy with the result or if it is manifestly unjust.

To arrange child support through the agency, you simply send in an application and the agreed amount will be docked from your pay. Otherwise, you can arrange to make the payments voluntarily.

Child support finishes at the age of eighteen but maintenance can continue for a child with an intellectual or physical health impediment for the rest of their days, and this also applies to children who need further education. So it is possible to get a maintenance order against a parent or both parents for a child over eighteen to go to university or for other tertiary education.

BE SAVVY ABOUT SUPER

As discussed earlier in this chapter, new rules from the end of 2002 covering superannuation in Australia allow for its division either by court order or mutual agreement in cases of separation. However, this varies depending on the type of scheme—that is, defined benefit or the more common accumulation fund.

Under the former legislation, impoverishment was sometimes forced on one partner for the short term, the other for the long term. The wife may have ended up with the house, the husband the superannuation. The new rules may mean that, while the wife gets a share of the superannuation, she will have to rehouse herself in the immediate future.

With this shakeup in superannuation, both parties can make sensible decisions, provided they work together. According to Benjamin:

> For example, if a couple breaks up with two children aged five and seven, the mother may be given a 65–35 property split. Under the change to the Act, the husband may say: 'I will rent for the next ten years and when the children grow up and the property is sold we will split the proceeds 50–50.' Under this scenario, they may both get a share of the superannuation.
>
> At least it will mean that the person not in the home will still get the capital appreciation while providing for the children. Because the father is providing a house, he may be able to apply to the Child Support Agency to reduce child support.

Those with a Reasonable Benefits Limit problem surrounding their taxation (see Chapter 12) can help eliminate their liability by splitting their superannuation on divorce and giving the excess component to their ex-spouse.

De facto couples should be aware that they do not get the same superannuation benefits because their rights fall under state, not federal, laws.

LEGAL AID

Broadly speaking, if you are arguing about a valuable inner-city property, you can forget about legal aid. In fact, if you jointly own any property of significance, you will be hard pressed to qualify for assistance. If you are unsure whether you would qualify for assistance, visit www.legalaid.com.au or phone the Legal Aid Helpline toll-free on 1800 806 913.

FAMILY TRUSTS

Contrary to popular opinion, assets cannot be hidden in family trusts. If an ex-husband has parked money in a family trust, then claims he has no say in its control—even though his siblings are trustees—a court will look at this long and hard and may easily find that he does have some control. If that's the outcome, the court will set it aside as a device, according to Benjamin:

> There have been a couple of cases where people have in fact transferred their assets to their accountants, where the accountant has said: 'Yes, that's fine, thank you for the asset.' If you alienate it too far then you've got to try to get the asset back.

PERSONAL GIFTS

If someone leaves you money during a marriage, it is classed as a matrimonial asset and will form part of the property pool as it has been accumulated during the marriage. The carve-up of this money will depend on where it came from, contributions and future needs.

For example, if my husband's maiden aunt leaves him $100 000 the day after I leave him, I won't have a big claim on that from a contribution point of view. If, however, that is his only asset and I have two small children, a court may say my contributions are nil but my future needs are significant so I will receive a share of that inheritance.

Other issues come into play. For example, I may have been good to his aunt, taken her shopping, cared for her when she was sick, and so on. These contributions will also be considered by a court.

If you are in a de facto or same-sex relationship and both earn similar incomes, your partner will have little entitlement to any gifted money as in such cases future needs are not taken into account.

SAME-SEX COUPLES

When it comes to property, same-sex couples are usually treated in the same manner as de factos. Once again, it will depend on your state laws. If Ned is in a relationship with Tom, and Ned goes out to work while Tom stays at home, preparing meals, providing a household environment and doing all the things expected of a partner at home, his contribution is taken into account, irrespective of gender. Benjamin says:

> If I've gone into the relationship with $1 million worth of assets and come out with $1 million, my partner can come along and say: 'Look, I've contributed to the maintenance of that property, the conservation of that property', and claim a share. The courts look at the length of time of the relationship, the type of contribution that was made, and out of all of those things they make a determination as to what share of that de facto or same-sex partnership they are entitled to receive.
>
> Under some state de facto laws, same-sex couples have a right to get a share. But if there is no contribution then they don't get a share. Say, for example, if I were in a de facto relationship for two years and I provided all of the contributions and my partner provided nothing then their contributions are nil.

Just remember, when love goes wrong you should do everything in your power to avoid expensive, lengthy court battles. They will not only eat away at your assets, but their outcome may not bring you happiness—even if you win.

Conclusion

When I asked a friend—a hopeless saver—to review my budgeting chapter, she jumped at the chance. 'I need all the help I can get and more,' she said laughing. A few days later, she called me to say she had cancelled her cable TV subscription because she and her husband never watched it, they were rethinking their second phone line and were even weighing up whether to manage with just one mobile rather than two.

This was great news. This was the sort of reaction I was hoping to receive from this book, as my aim was to provide plenty of commonsense information on a range of subjects such as goal-setting, getting out of debt, financial planning, property, investment, insurance, tax, superannuation and wills that may help you as a couple on the road to wealth creation.

I was also hoping to drive home the message of the importance of doing your research. And that applies to big and small investments—from a managed fund to a mobile phone. Rather than just take the easy route, shop around and make sure whatever you are spending your money on is the best possible vehicle for you.

Another issue which seems to be close to many couples' hearts is dealing with emotions from past relationships. Children and ex-partners are an ever-present reminder of the age we live in. The most important point to remember is that no matter what has happened in the past, the children always come first. I feel very strongly about this, having two wonderful stepchildren of my own. Another important thing to remember is that almost every problem has a solution. Finding it is just a matter of good and open communication.

Setting yourself up for the future takes planning and patience. If you have spent your twenties spending up big and having a great time, don't despair—it's not too late to take control. With two of you hellbent on succeeding, and with clear and agreed goals, you can't lose.

Just remember to enjoy your life together along the way and never forget that the journey you take, not where you end up, is the reward.

Appendix 1: Personal Money Plan

Income	
Net Take Home Pay	$
	$
Social Security Payment	$
Family Payment	$
Maintenance Received	$
Board Received	$
AUSTUDY	$
Other Income	$
Total Income	**$**

Summary	
Total Income (as above)	$
Less Total Basic Living Costs	$
Subtotal	**$**
Less Repayments	$
Surplus or (Deficit)	**$**

Expenditure Sheet

HOUSING	
Rent	$
1st Mortgage	$
2nd Mortgage	$
Land Rates	$
Insurance	$
House Repairs	$
Strata Levies	$
Home Replacements	$
UTILITIES	
Electricity	$
Heating Oil	$
Gas	$
Water	$
Telephone/mobile	$
Internet/Pay TV	$
TRANSPORT	
Petrol	$
Repairs	$
Registration	$
CTP Green Slip	$
Insurance	$
NRMA/Licence	$
Fares	$
FOOD	
Groceries	$
Meat	$
Fruit & Vegetables	$
Milk	$
Bread	$
Lunches	$
Pet Food	$
Take Away Food	$
EDUCATION	
School Fees	$
Uniforms	$
Tutoring/Books	$
Sports	$
Pre-school	$
Child Minding	$
MEDICAL	
Fund Contributions	$
Doctor	$
Dentist	$
Chemist	$
Optometrist	$
Specialist	$
Vet Fees/Pet Costs	$
SUBTOTAL CARRIED FORWARD	$

Subtotal brought forward	$
PERSONAL	
Clothing	$
Haircuts	$
Grooming/Cosmetics	$
Entertainment	$
Sport	$
Club Fees	$
Newspaper & Magazines	$
Holiday Savings	$
Gifts/Xmas/Birthdays etc	$
Pocket Money	$
Alcohol	$
Cigarettes/Tobacco	$
Laundry/Dry Cleaning	$
Gambling Lotto/Other	$
Donations Church/Other	$
Videos/Movies	$
Postage/Films	$
Pool/Gardening Expenses	$
OTHER	
Child Support/ Maintenance	$
Taxation	$
Superannuation	$
Other Expenditure	$
Savings	$
Special Project	$
TOTAL BASIC LIVING COSTS	
REPAYMENTS	
Bank Credit Cards	$
Credit Union	$
Store Accounts	$
Finance Companies	$
Rental/Lease	$
Car Loan	$
Taxation	$
Pawnbrokers	$
Family/Friends	$
Other Lenders	$
TOTAL REPAYMENTS	$
TOTAL ALL EXPENDITURE	$

Source: Ryde-Eastwood Financial Counselling Service

Index

accountants 21, 150–1
accumulation funds 167
addictions 44–5
assets 79
attitudes 14–15
auctions 99–100
Australian Stock Exchange (ASX) 132–3

baby bonus 154
bank accounts 56, 81–3
bankruptcy 48
bonds 115, 127–8
broking accounts 136–7
budgets
- children's education 62–4
- credit costs 60–2
- double incomes 51–2
- drawing up 52–4
- mobile phones 58–60
- saving 54–5
- spending 50–1
- tips 56–8
- trigger for 50

buy-back offers 135

capital gains tax (CGT) 146–7, 156–7
cars 57, 69, 156
cash investments 114
child care 72–3, 153
child maintenance 84–7
child support 210
children
- costs of 70–2, 74–5, 86–8
- from previous relationships 83–7

Christmas 46–7
co-borrowing 35–8
company funds 165
compound interest 122–4
compromise 78
consolidation accounts 175–6
conveyancing 101
costings 18
credit cards 40, 57–8, 60–1
credit rating 42

de facto couples 194–5, 207–10
debentures 115
debt
- addictions 44–5
- affect on health 33
- bankruptcy 48
- Christmas 46–7
- credit cards 40
- household 33
- impulse buying 38–9
- incurring 35
- interest rates 44
- joint 35–8
- living beyond your means 42–3
- mobile phones 42

partner's 45–6
reducing 43–4
serious 34
sexually transmitted 35–8
store cards 41–2
defined benefit funds 167
deposit bonds 104–5
discount brokers 134–5
diversification 90, 110, 127–8, 134, 138
dividend imputation 147–8
divorce
assets and liabilities 199–200
child support 210
counselling 198
court appearances 203, 205
de facto couples 207–10
family trusts 212
joint assets 201
legal aid 211
online settlement 202–3
out of court settlement 206–7
personal gifts 212
priorities 201–2
property settlements 203–4, 206
same-sex couples 212–13
settlement timing 206
solicitors 198–9
superannuation 210–11
dollar-cost averaging 128–9
dreams 13–14

earning power 2
education 62–4
emerging markets 120
emotional baggage 77–88
end-of-year tax schemes 152–3
ethical funds 119–20
executors 190–1
expenses 53, 66

family history 14
family tax benefits 153
family trusts 157–8, 212
fees 61, 69
financial advisers 17, 129
changing 27–8
costs 24
finding 21–2, 28
interviewing 23
making demands 26–7
questions for 28
reviews 27
risk 26
sharing goals 24–6
financial dependence 70
financial personalities 6–12
Financial Planning Association (FPA) 22
financial plans 25–6
fixed interest investments 114–15
franked dividends 147–8
fringe benefits tax (FBT) 148, 152

goals
accomplishing 2
chart 18
costings 18
defining 15–17
discussing 24–5
getting started 6–19
limiting 18
setting 5, 15–18, 54
grocery shopping 69
growth assets 126–7, 168–70
guarantors 35, 37

health 33

high risk investments 125–6
home contents insurance 184–7
home loan redraw 38
home loans 91–5
home offices 154–6

impulse buying 38–9
income protection insurance 76, 179–81
incomes 51–2
  child care 72–3
  children 70–2, 74–5
  financial dependence 70
  income protection insurance 76
  mortgage repayments 68–70
  single 66–76
  splitting 143–5
industry funds 163
initial public offerings (IPOs) 137
insurance
  home contents 184–7
  income protection 179–81
  life 177–8
  private health 181–3
  total and permanent disability (TPD) 180
  trauma 183–4
interest rates 40, 44
investments
  cash 114
  choices 114
  compound interest 122–4
  diversification 127–8
  dollar-cost averaging 128–9
  emerging markets 120
  fixed interest 114–15
  frequent 5
  growth assets 126–7
  high risk 125–6
  income splitting 143–5
  long-term 124–5
  managed funds 117–19
  market crashes 124–5
  master trusts 120–1
  property 89–112
  shares 116–17
  socially responsible (SRIs) 119–20
  starting 122
  superannuation 159–76
  tax deductions 142–3
  timing 124
  tips 122–9
  wrap services 121

joint accounts 37, 81–3
joint assets 201
joint tenants 102, 196

legal aid 211
legalities 101–2
life insurance 177–8
lifestyle 2, 23, 57
listed property trusts (LPTs) 109–12

managed funds 26, 117–19
margin calls 140–1
margin lending 140
market crashes 124–5
master funds 163–5
master trusts 120–1
mobile phones 42, 58–60, 69
money quarrels 3–4
mortgage assistance 68
mortgage brokers 94–5
mortgage insurance 91
mortgage offset accounts 147
mortgage repayments 58, 68–70, 95–7, 102

negative gearing 103, 132, 145–6
non-conforming lenders 112

offset accounts 147
online banking 56, 57, 69
online divorce settlement 202–3
over-capitalisation 107–8

personal gifts 212
personalities 6–12
plans 5
pre-nuptial agreements 79–81
private health insurance 69, 181–3
property 57, 83
  auctions 99–100
  deposit bonds 104–5
  deposits 90–1
  dream home 97–8
  home loans 91–5
  investment 102–4
  joint names 209–10
  joint tenants 102
  legalities 101–2
  listed property trusts 109–12
  making an offer 100–1
  mortgage repayments 95–7, 102
  off the plan 104
  purchasing 105–9
  renovating 107–9
  renting 105–7
  research 98–9
  tenants in common 102
property settlements 203–4, 206
public trustee 191, 193

quarrels 3–4

reasonable benefit limits (RBLs) 172
redraw facility 112
reinvestment 122–4
renovations 107–9
renting 55, 105–7
research 98–9, 130
retirement 80, 160, 161, 167–76
risk 26

salary packaging 148–9
salary sacrificing 151–2, 172
sales 56
same-sex couples 194–5, 212–13
saving 3–4, 5, 7, 50–1, 54–5, 56, 90–1
savvy personalities 8
school fees 69
self-employment 176
self-managed funds 166–7
sexually transmitted debt 35–8
shares 116–17, 127–8
  broking accounts 136–7
  buy-back offers 135
  buying 131–2, 133–4, 139
  discount brokers 134–5
  diversification 134, 138
  initial public offerings (IPOs) 137
  joint loans 132
  joint names 131
  margin calls 140–1
  margin lending 140
  profit objectives 136
  selecting 132–3
  selling 134, 136–7
  stop-loss position 134, 136
  tips for buying 136–40
shopping around 56, 69
socially responsible investments (SRIs) 119–20
spending 3–4, 50–1
stamp duty 110

steady personalities 8
stockbrokers 21
store cards 41–2
superannuation 127
  accumulation funds 167
  combined incomes 162–3
  company funds 165
  consolidation 175–6
  defined benefit funds 167
  division of 210–11
  growth assets 168–70
  industry funds 163
  levels 161–2
  long-term 170
  master funds 163–5
  personal plans 165
  reasonable benefit limits (RBLs) 172
  salary sacrificing 172
  self-managed 166–7
  spouse contributions 172–4
  tax benefits 160–1, 171–2
  undeducted contributions 174
sustainable wealth 5

taxation
  accountants 150–1
  baby bonus 154
  cars 156
  capital gains (CGT) 146–7, 156–7
  claims 154–5
  dividend imputation 147–8
  end-of-year schemes 152–3
  family benefits 153
  family trusts 157–8
  franked dividends 147–8
  fringe benefits (FBT) 148, 152
  home offices 154–6
  income splitting 143–5
  negative gearing 145–6
  offset accounts 147
  planning professionals 149–50
  returns 151
  salary packaging 148–9
  salary sacrificing 151–2
  superannuation 160–1, 171–2
  wills 188–9
teamwork 5
technology boom 139
tenants in common 102, 196
term deposits 115
thrillseekers 7–8
timidity 8
total and permanent disability (TPD) insurance 180
trauma insurance 183–4
trusts 193–4

undeducted contributions 174
unsecured notes 115

values 13

wages *see* incomes
wealth 5
wills
  contesting 194
  costs 191–3
  drawing up 189–90
  dying intestate 190
  executors 190–1
  inheritance 194–5
  revocation 193
  safekeeping 194
  trusts 193–4
wrap services 121